Guide Your Career

by

Seamus Whitney

with Suzanne Power

Version1.0 – October 2017

Website: www.whitneycareerguidance.com

ISBN: 978-1978402188

This book is not designed to provide psychological advice or as a substitute for professional counselling. The information comes with no warranty, expressed or implied, with regard to the subject matter. It is sold with the understanding that the authors are not engaged in rendering legal, accounting, medical or other professional advice. If legal advice or other professional assistance is required, the services of a competent professional should be sought. Seamus Whitney & Suzanne Power, individually or corporately, do not accept any responsibility for any liabilities resulting from the actions of any parties involved. No responsibility is accepted for use of this information. Use is entirely at your own risk. Information contained is for educational purposes only.

Front Cover: Painting by John Hesnan, inspired by artist G.C. Myer's image 'Siddhartha', www.gcmyers.com, New York.

Contents

Acknowledgements

To Suzanne Power, a writer, mentor and editor, for the unceasing support and belief that she has in me, not just in co-writing and developing this book, but also in the work that I do.

To all those wonderful people who came forward to have their stories told and included in this book. I have great admiration for you.

To the many clients and their parents that have trusted me with their career progression plans to date. It has been a privilege to have been allowed to guide along the path. I could not imagine how empty my life would have been without meeting and working with you all.

To my family for their unwavering support over the past twenty years. Nothing is ever too much to ask for, and I greatly appreciate all the help.

To Mary Hickey, thank you for being a rock of support for me in Whitney Career Guidance. You have been an ever-present inspiration for me over the past ten years.

To Brid Colloton, thank you for all the work you do and for being the gel that holds Whitney Career Guidance together. I hope you continue to grow and expand your role within the company.

To John Hesnan, my publisher. Thanks for showing up in my life just at the right time John. I wish you well in your future endeavours both as a publisher and a careers advisor.

To Laura Codd for her dedicated work and good cheer, and without whom this manuscript would not have been possible.

To G.C. Myers, www.gcmyers.com, New York, for his permission to use the reproductions of his painting 'Siddhartha'.

Acknowledgements

To all my friends in the various spiritual groups that I am involved with. I hope that you continue to work miracles for all.

To my parents Jim and Eileen, it is only becoming apparent now how much you gave to us all as a family.

To Nuala and all at Evolv who keep me functioning so well on the physical level.

To all at Wexford Enterprise Centre and Wexford Local Enterprise Office for playing such an influential role in getting my business established.

To Niall Reck and all at Graphedia, your creativity and passion for helping have given us all at Whitney Career Guidance a huge lift this year.

Everybody needs good friends, and I am very lucky to have two of the best in Alan and Butch.

Finally, if I have worked with you as a colleague or socialised with you as a friend, if you have been a teammate or a volunteer alongside me throughout my life, then thanks a million...... you have helped me become the person that I am today.

Website: https://www.whitneycareerguidance.com/

Introduction

Listening to the Quiet Revolution

 Why am I writing this a book about careers? There was never any indication in my early years that I would ever be giving this kind of guidance to people. I didn't have any particular gift for helping people to make career decisions. Teaching in the formal sense was never likely. The largest part of my working life was in large manufacturing companies. So how did all of this come about?

I am a listener. But for myself, I didn't hear the messages or see the signs, because I hadn't set out to be a careers advisor.

It was a role that kept calling me.

First of all, it happened on an informal basis with colleagues in manufacturing. Then I was sent for training, which led to training others in-house. This led to part-time external consultancy and the sudden realisation, decades in the making, that the world of work was changing at the most rapid rate since industrialisation, and there was no one to tell the past worker where to go in the present marketplace. There was no guidance for what future opportunities could be made.

I just filled a gaping hole in the system, before I even realised the hole was there, on an ad hoc basis. This invited me to listen to my own opportunity. The questions others asked began to prompt my own:

What do I most want to do? Where can I find the work that will most suit me? What do I have to do to get it?

There were, are, still few answers to these questions that are informed, cohesive and qualified. I began to gather the information on the Irish work marketplace and centres of education into a full resource. Along with centralising the information, I began to put

Introduction

together methods of self-enquiry to get the individual to think for themselves, of themselves.

This is what I call listening to the quiet revolution – people, singly or in groups when made redundant or meeting in classrooms or employment centres – turning inward to find the outward road they want to take in their working life.

It is a practice that is becoming more common, being met by far from perfect advice – at best patchy and at worst outdated.

For this process to truly flourish, guidance is a great start on a new path or to enhance a present career path.

I grew into my own role, one conversation at a time. The conversations became interviews, the interviews became reviews and the reviews became consultations which in turn offered counselling aspects.

I use the term career guidance counsellor as it is the accepted title of the role, but career guide is what I titled the book as and what I think is more appropriate. It is simpler on the tongue and the concept is the same. It's your career; I guide, but you steer.

For over twenty years I have been showing up and answering the questions that people can't seem to find answers for. Principally I am an information giver, and I am always amazed as to why this critical service is not more freely available in this country today. Another source of amazement is the array of poor quality, and expensive, aptitude tests that people trust to guide their entire futures.

This led me down the road of developing my own set of assessment tools. After ten or more years I finally arrived at a set of assessments that I now feel meet the needs of people about to make major life-changing career decisions.

This book speaks about the process of career guidance for people of all ages. This is not a traditional career guidance manual, detailing endless lists of colleges and courses. Rather it looks at the issues around you guiding yourself (or your children) through the various factors that have a major influence on choosing careers or college courses.

I look closely at factors such as motivation, destiny, decision-making, as well as the very important role that parents play in influencing their children's career choices.

To help illustrate how all of this works, I have included a number of client case studies reflecting the various trials and challenges people face every day in relation to finding the work and career that suits them most. The names of the people have been changed to protect their anonymity.

People come to me from ages 15 to 50 plus. They all have the same questions. They all are affected by the same stress and are all seeking to take the next step in their career. The differences are linked to the life-stage each individual has reached. Factors that motivate a 17-year-old boy or girl are obviously very different to factors that may influence the decisions of an adult at age 40.

Whatever the age, the ultimate task for the career guide is always the same - to provide the environment and facilitate the enlarging of perspective which allows that person to reflect accurately on their needs and desires. We strive to help them make a decision that allows them to grow and evolve in a holistic manner, so that they may reach the highest potential, be the best person they can be in their life.

Work has become a huge part of our everyday lives. An entity we consider as well as we do to survive. Work has become an extension of us.

There are documented and obvious benefits associated with being content in work or having a sense of purpose in a career. However when a person is forced to work in a job or carry out a role they are unhappy with, they often find that they are drained of energy, are under constant stress and are suffering from anxiety.

In short, they are barely surviving.

There is little or no time for growth and development for the person caught in these situations. Helping them break free is a key function of the career guide. This is a function that takes time and patience. These critical components of career guidance sadly are lacking in Ireland today. It begins at 17, and we are still making errors we know the consequences of with our future workforce. A recent survey found that 65 percent of the jobs our school children will do have not even been invented yet.

Introduction

Because of the upsurge in new technologies and social media, young people may have more opportunities but face many more challenges than our generation did. Another factor arising from recent research is that of those people who don't progress in their chosen college courses, who underperform or even drop out, two out of three of these students feel the main reason for non-progression was that they didn't fit in.

We do not prepare our young people for the imminent challenges that lie ahead as they line up to leave home. I often have to ask parents to see their children no longer as their children but to remember the children they once were.

What goes on in the minds of our young people? The answer is we don't know. Sometimes we think our children have it all together and sometimes we expect them to act and behave in a certain way, based on everything we have told them. But just take it back to that time when you were 18. You thought you knew everything, but actually, you were very bereft of the necessary experience and resilience that you needed to function in the world. Added to this there are very important factors for young students that can play a big role in their everyday college lives. But not necessarily contribute to their adult ones.

Questions such as *can I make the college team/get selected for that part at the audition?* often outweigh the importance of securing grades and completing assignments.

Then there is the social scene. I am always amazed to hear that many drinks companies deliberately target the student market and run their promotions on Monday evenings! What a promising start to the academic week. It's no wonder that surviving modern college social life can be a real problem.

The major point here is that young people are not equipped to face the challenges that the modern college and early work environment throw at them. I will focus on early work issues in the forthcoming chapters. The issue with education affects careers almost at once. When it comes to our young people, there are major flaws in the education and guidance systems which are not being addressed.

The emphasis of their preparation is almost entirely on the academic front, and virtually no thought or action is given to getting the student ready for the emotional upheaval that moving away to college can bring. Protected from these challenges by *helicopter parenting* while still at home, they are often left to go it alone once they step on campus.

If you think that this book is an attack on the guidance services provided in secondary schools, then it is not. Career guidance at second level while important, can in a lot of cases be just the starting point for a person's career. The leap from school to college is out of one galaxy into another. The point's race is missing the point. While you're racing to get qualifications you're not qualified to make the right decisions with them.

In my view, the focus of giving career guidance today seems to be one of providing masses of data both online and through college prospectuses. This has the effect of confusing people. They often ring me in desperation, totally lost and bewildered. Of course what they need is someone to talk face to face with, time to ask their questions so their fears may be allayed, but this much-needed service is almost non-existent in our country.

There seems to be a huge void in the provision of quality career guidance within education and employment, and this includes services for adults. This has been caused mainly by the lack of a cohesive approach to this hugely important area. It is a known fact that one in six students will drop out of college in their first year at the cost of around €35 million to the country. This financial cost is huge, but the knock-on emotional cost is indeterminable. From where I'm sitting nobody seems to have overall responsibility, so the financial and emotional haemorrhage continues.

Other countries do care and have the systems and resources in place to address this need. One of my hopes for writing this book is that it might be a catalyst for positive change; it might start a conversation that may eventually lead to a realisation that something needs to be done.

Career pathways have become very complex in recent years and are likely to become more and more complex in the future. Everybody realises that the job for life scenario is well and truly gone, with people now expecting to have two to three major career changes in their working lives. The expectation that you will be well qualified to match the quicksilver market is higher than ever, and will not diminish.

Having the right qualifications for a successful career can also be a daunting challenge. Indeed Ireland has become a qualification driven country. I remember twenty years ago when people started to arrive from Eastern Europe. I was always amazed at the level of qualifications they possessed. Many had Master's degrees but had struggled to get work in their native countries, so took menial jobs in Ireland to make a lot more money than they could at home.

At that time I never believed that a similar situation would exist in Ireland just a short while later, but it does. Now even the most basic employment seems to require almost a degree level standard. Many of the more prestigious jobs and careers require young people to spend endless years in college and university, gaining the necessary qualifications sometimes at great expense to their poor parents.

When I left college with a Higher Certificate in Chemistry back in the 1970's, I had exceeded the level of education that the vast majority of my peers had at that time. Through hard work determination and probably a bit of luck, I managed to create a very varied and successful career. It just wouldn't be possible now; my CV wouldn't get a look in. It's sad really, but it seems like our individual talent and drive doesn't matter so much anymore. Nowadays career progression is all about how far you can progress along the National Framework of Qualifications.

Having said this, a PhD is worthless without self-knowledge.

There is a quiet revolution underway, and I have spent two decades seeing signs on the horizon of what might occur if the future got faster and more personal at the same time. It has. We need to work harder than ever, and so we have to be most ourselves, and that is the message of this book.

Individual needs and expression are not luxuries in the modern economy – they are essentials. Read on to find your potential contribution. Find out how to be most yourself at work so that you have the energy and insight for challenges and opportunities to come. Get that combination right, and you will be not only a player but a part of it.

1

LIFE LESSONS

Chapter 1

Life Lessons

Working out your Combination

'Choose a job you love, and you will never have to work a day in your life.'
Confucius

 You can't provide guidance unless you've made the errors and learned from them. My working life has been a combination of faith, chance happenings and self-determination. Throw in a quandary, finding focus through difficult situations, and, at one point, the overriding smell of ammonia, to get the full sensory impact.

Negotiating a career, not knowing what lies ahead, is a bit like trying to open a combination lock with no idea what digits will work.

You have to keep trying.

The first digit of the code of my combination lock is *seventy-four*. I sat my Leaving Cert in 1974. At the time, there was really no career guidance in existence in any school. The only guidance was to make sure we passed the Leaving Cert. Plus: *don't fail maths*! We were warned '*if you fail maths you fail the whole thing*'. Now for a student like myself at the time, weak at maths and with very low motivation for school, this was a troubling scenario, one that caused me a great deal of anxiety.

14

Chapter 1 – Life Lessons

In the absence of grind schools or private colleges, there was only one strategy for me really to pass that Leaving Cert: To pray hard, very hard!

So, every morning from Ash Wednesday right through to the morning of my final examination, I got out of that bed early and made my way down to the local church. Diligently attending eight o'clock morning mass and praying like hell was coming for me that I would pass maths and get that Cert.

Fast forward onto August. Results came in, and to my great surprise and relief, I managed to just about pass. I had my Leaving Cert, which was fine. All of a sudden it dawned on me: What was I going to do next?

The next digit in my career path combination is a big *zero*. Zero preparation, zero input from others, zero ideas of what was ahead. All my focus, all my praying, had been for something right in front of me. The future after it, obscured by the mushroom cloud of anxiety around the exam everyone talked about. So I went straight into anti-climax, and a new stretch of fear opened up to replace the objective. On the day I heard I made it, I began to realise I hadn't even begun to.

A space began to clear around me. Some of my closest friends had moved onto jobs with *An Post* and the *ESB*, but I was left hanging until the last week of August with no real idea of what to do.

My parents couldn't help either; they watched me watch other school companions move onto the future I needed to occupy. It was a low time. What should have been the best summer of my life was washed out with last-minute cramming for new avenues for study or work. I think in desperation my father said:

'I heard a new college is opening up in Carlow. Maybe we should go up and take a look.'

A man with no Leaving Cert was advising the son with the magic piece of paper.

The idea of going to college was completely alien to me at the time. With no CAO, no career guidance and no common sense, no mentors who could advise me on how to proceed, my first awareness that everyone needs proper guidance at this crucial juncture formed. It was this consternation that gave me the seeds of an idea I would not put into practice for nearly twenty years. But in those early year and fears, I found my truth path. The young man was asking:

Would I apply? What would I study? Where would I live?

These were all questions that were racing through my mind as we took the road to Carlow, which was long and winding at the time.

When we got there, we were met at the door by a lecturer called Dr Jimmy Parkes, and Jimmy's opening comments to me were:

'Hi Seamus, you're welcome here. C'mon upstairs and I'll show you where you're going to be studying Science.' And that was it.

He told me, who up to an hour previously was full of uncertainty, the certain fact that I was starting lectures the following Monday. I was signed up for a course in applied chemistry.

Chemistry! I'd barely scraped through ordinary level chemistry in the Leaving, and I had failed physics! If Seamus is from Mars, then chemistry is from another galaxy, far far away. Not just something I had never considered, something that should not have even been in my universe.

However, in the absence of any direction or alternative route, it was my only option.

I turned up and signed up for an initial two-year Certificate in Applied Chemistry.

Two, the next click in my lock. Two more years of my life. I hated every minute of it. Between the labs, the hours, the library work I really struggled. Although I was only up the road in Carlow, I was very homesick and missed all my friends.

Ten, the number came quickly. Basketball – my saviour at the time and in subsequent years. Five guys on court, plus five benched, all learning from each other. Only for my love of playing basketball, I would have dropped out by Christmas. I was lucky enough to meet a group of lads from the Midlands who shared my passion. I signed up for the college team and learned so much from those guys. I had a great couple of years with them, and we actually won the All-Ireland College's title in my second year of studies. That was a real highlight for me. Ten Happy Men.

Chapter 1 – Life Lessons

Nineteen. I turned nineteen, my next number; not receiving a hero's welcome but deserving of one after the hard slog. I sat my final exams in May. Following these, I got offered a position in *Cow & Gate,* the baby food manufacturers, in Wexford.

Twenty. I worked as a laboratory technician during the summer, happy there despite the low wage of £20 a week. The next number in the combination. My first pay packet was a pound over my age. What was priceless was that I got on well with all the staff. They offered me a position to stay on at the end of the holidays.

The crossroads opened up again. I took the opportunity to work, as opposed to going back to college and by Christmas, I had landed myself a better job in IFI, a very large manufacturer of fertiliser, in Arklow at the time.

I was very excited about working for IFI. I thought I might get to use some of the Chemistry I had studied in college, but I was really unhappy. I never really adjusted to the twelve-hour shifts, in particular, the nights which I found really difficult.

My immune system ran down. The abiding memory I have is the smell of ammonia. They say smelling is the sense with the longest memory. I thought I had finished up with ammonia in the college labs. Here I was, drowning in an ammonia tsunami. If you haven't smelled it, well, it's almost equivalent to the worst public toilet smell on a humid, windless summer day.

I can't use the same numbers twice, but again I have to try *two*, even though I have a prevailing sense it is isn't working. I put in two more years for something I hated, as I hated my college course. Circumstances are different but never the same. I did another stretch before the resignation letter brought my life and nose a great relief.

The new position was a lifesaver at Life Savers Manufacturing, a new US Confectionary company who had moved to Wexford to make, of all things, bubble-gum.

Pop went that dream all over my face. Good things come to an end. A very sudden end. Due to a huge overestimation of the European market, Life Savers were left with a warehouse full of unsold bubble-gum and, in their wisdom, they decided to close the operation after a mere fifteen months.

You can't feed a family on bubble-gum. I got work doing anything at all. After brief stints in sales positions and working on construction sites, my next role came into view making optical spectacle lenses. Another start-up company in Wexford, this one had done their market research and were manufacturing what was needed.

They were growing fast and offered me the job as Quality Assurance Supervisor, which I gladly took. Having had five jobs in as many years, I was hoping to get another year or two out of this company, but then I found another number to unlock my personal career combination.

Seventeen. I was to spend a further seventeen years with this organisation. It was to become a major influence in my working career. Up to then, my work life had proved an uneventful routine, mainly providing a salary for me to fund my lifestyle.

Twenty. I call this period The Roaring Twenties – I spent most of my decade roaring and shouting at young people to train harder and play better. My life was basketball. Coaching young people was a big passion.

Thirty. Things are changing, the lock is still tight, but the number feels right. As I approached my thirtieth birthday, after five years of working with the company, I began to sense an unease within me. The routine had become almost unbearable.

Days and weeks were dragging out, and I felt I needed something more.

This number is too long to try, but that's because it was the longest recession of the twentieth century. The year 1980 dawned very dark and stayed that way for a decade. It saw very few companies hiring. There was nowhere to go. The only progress I could make was within my current company. I had a chat with my manager at the time, and we had a look around for some courses that might give my sagging career the lift it needed.

The best thing we could come up with was a course in Quality Assurance at the then College of Commerce in Rathmines, Dublin. Now metamorphosed into DIT Aungier Street, back then the only technical aspect was the giant clock presiding over the town. I thought about it, decided I needed to do something, and headed off.

Expect the unexpected when you meet lecturers, and your name is Seamus Whitney. I arrived there on a bright Monday morning, very enthusiastic, to meet our main lecturer. He informed the small group that this course was 90 percent maths and statistics! I stared at the exit door and decided to run for it. I sat tight and waited for the break, so I could make mine.

As the morning wore on, I considered the variables, with everything in place and accommodation fixed, I couldn't run and hide. My only option was to give it a try and see. I sat close to the front, and I eyeballed the lecturer (who in fairness was very good at his job), and I surprised myself by understanding a lot of the concepts he was trying to teach us.

This is another aspect of our journey together through this book. There is nothing like experience to teach you what you need to know. I had developed into someone who had assimilated on the job context for a subject that baffled me while it remained on paper.

I saw how I needed to have a better understanding of statistics in particular, as they were widely used in the sampling plans we were using in Quality Assurance.

Now there are too many numbers to list, but I knew them, finally for the first time in my life. I worked day and night with numbers. Lots of them.

As you will learn what combination works for you by trial and error, so I found my trials and errors were paying off in this new approach. I studied by day, did my homework assignments by night, and felt ready and confident for the exams once they came around. When we got the results, I opened the letter with great trepidation, but was delighted and surprised that my grade was a Distinction.

'How come?' I asked. I was the same person who had scraped the minimum D on the ordinary Leaving Cert paper ten years previously.

I learned some very valuable life lessons from that experience.

The last numbers of the lock were simple, and it finally released. They are numbers we all share. *As simple as one, two, three.*

Number 1: There was a big difference in me as a learner at seventeen and twenty-seven.

Number 2: The motivation to learn is the key thing, and in my view, it is the most important study skill. If you don't have the motivation to take in what the teacher/lecturer is trying to tell you, most information goes over your head. Subsequent attempts to revise and recap are often futile.

Number 3: If you're a potential mature student, thinking maybe of going back to college, but nervous because you had, like me, a very average Leaving Cert - don't let that put you off. Mature students make excellent learners, colleges know this, and that's why they welcome them with open arms.

If you're thinking about it, just do it! You could be like me and be pleasantly surprised by the outcome.

So there it is. My lock snapped open, but I was still only halfway to learning what and who I was. Waiting beneath was a smaller lock, requiring more thought and needing a key this time. The key was given to me, but how I placed it in the mechanism, how I turned it, was vital. Action was everything now. The action I took benefiting from my previous experience, offering more questions and providing answers that came from living my way into them.

I turned the key to my next phase of living and working.

When the student is ready, the teacher appears.

Armed with new skills and knowledge, I quickly applied my learning to the work situation and began to see improvements all round in the process. This gave me the confidence to search for new skills. I made contact with what was the Irish Quality Association at the time and convinced my company to apply for the new Quality Mark, which at the time was quite prestigious. Within twelve months of making the application and the successful audit, the company were awarded the Mark, quite new for a company like the one I worked for.

At this time I felt people started to take a bit more notice of my work and wanted more. This prompted me to convince them to go for a much more complex certification IS9002 (very new and not a lot of people knew how to get this at the time). We worked hard, and after a couple of years we managed to pass this audit and again were awarded certification. The Wexford plant was the first division within the international company to be awarded this.

Now I felt people began to take notice internationally. The young lad clutching the Leaving Cert, heading up a winding road to Carlow, to see a college his father had read about, to study something he had no initial aptitude for, was now offered a position based on having initiated, executed and achieved a global standard.

A significant promotion followed. Shortly afterwards I was invited to be the Ireland representative on the International Standards Organisation Committee for Optical Lenses. Between travelling to meetings for this body and visiting our large company's European base, I was spending a lot of time away from home.

I had become the high-flying executive (full of my own importance of course), and I noticed that my basketball coaching commitments were on the wane. I had a left a strand of myself behind. But I was in a bigger world.

What next? I had a hunger to keep moving forward, and the sky seemed to have no limits in terms of climbing the management ladder. The job offers came to keep me where I was. All I had to do was be patient and keep doing what I was doing. I waited to see what my next move might be. But what happened next astonished me.

I could never have predicted it in a million years.

Fully expecting a new Technical or Quality Role I was called in by the CEO and told that he wanted me to move to the brand new Human Resources Department he was setting up. Human Resources!

I had absolutely no experience or training in that area and was totally confused.

The company told me it would be a training and development role. My experience in project management and working with people in continuous improvement teams was the key to the success of this venture they said. And besides that, they saw I could take on new concepts and make them into realities.

They gave me time to consider an offer which came as a complete surprise.

I had a think about it. When I looked back on my life, up to this point, I saw it was always peppered with people. I was a leader in our local youth club from a very young age and had set up our local basketball club. I was a qualified coach. My passion was always working with people. And I had handled curved balls all my life:

Maths, Chemistry, Bubblegum, Fertiliser, Ammonia, Optical Lenses, Statistics, Quality Standards..

All the surprises had resulted in new opportunities. All of them had involved people. All of them had involved change. I was good, I realised, at change, people, motivation, work and challenge. So, without thinking too much more, I decided, yes, this might work too. It was a big change. I liked change then and I do still. I intuitively felt this might work out.

And within weeks I realised I had been in the wrong career for all of my previous working life!

I signed up for the new job on the condition that I would get significant training and was quickly dispatched off to the Irish Management Institute in Dublin for a major HR Development Programme. I started my new role in 1994. Within a very short period, I came to the realisation that HR was definitely the area for me. I settled quickly and well into it, was hungry for knowledge and devoured every piece of information I could get my hands on.

At the same time, I was gaining experience in all aspects of HR. Always conscious that I left full-time education a little prematurely, I was anxious to start another course. Returning to college on a full-time basis wasn't an option, so I signed up with the IMI/Henley College for a part-time Diploma in Management and started to study through distance learning.

Anyone who has ever studied remotely knows that it is not the remotest bit easy. I had a young family. It was a challenging time, and I found it difficult to balance my work/family commitments. But I got through it all and thankfully completed the course.

Needle in a Paper Mill - Assessing People's Work Interests in the Nineties.

In the mid-nineties, it was difficult to source any part-time or online education. With the internet in its infancy, we relied on sporadic brochures and communications from colleges or other institutions. To my memory, only DIT or UCD were offering any significant part-time education while, in the South East, WIT had just started to offer a limited range of programmes. Despite this, there seemed to be a hunger in people. They seemed to be waking up to the possibility of improving their education and career prospects. Many people were eager to engage in part-time learning.

At the time it seemed to be fashionable to study for a degree. Lots and lots of people were coming to me in HR to get advice from me about retraining.

While I felt I did my best to help people to find part-time courses, I found it extremely difficult to advise employees on which ones to take. If they didn't know themselves what they were suitable for, there was nothing available to help assess their interest or aptitude from a work perspective.

I searched high and low. The best that I could come up with was an outdated *Manual Interests Inventory*. This questionnaire, believe it or not, was completed by sticking pins into a paper answer form. I remember at the time before anybody completed it that I had to have a sheet of cardboard underneath the questionnaire, otherwise my desk would have been peppered with pin holes.

If you keep searching, if you keep looking beyond certainty for what might come next, you will find your learning opportunity. In 1996 I found Saville and Holdsworth Limited. SHL, as they were known at the time, had a whole battery of interests and assessment materials. I now felt I had something objective to measure people's career and work interests. I tried some of the tests with employees and people outside the company. They found them helpful in identifying which areas to pursue in career development.

Then the unexpected happened, again, and the next step began.

Many of the employees who came to me subsequently asked about advice for their children. The general consensus was that children weren't getting much career guidance in school. This surprised me, as I thought the education system had moved on from my experience. However, this insight was not lost on me, and I stored the information away until I was clearer about my future direction.

Besides, I had a day job to hold down, so I held it and spent three to four years working in the various departments within HR. Shortly afterwards the senior HR manager announced he was leaving. I felt this was a great opportunity for me to take a big step on the career ladder. At the time I was approaching another milestone birthday: 40.

I thought that now I was finally going to get the big move that I had worked so hard for over the past number of years. As it turned out, I was going to get my move alright, but on this occasion, life had a completely different plan than the one I thought was imminent.

I had been doing some private assessments on a part-time basis, mainly to try out the new techniques I had trained on; wanting to see what feedback, outside the company environment was, to the approaches I was both researching and formulating

At the time I had no real intention of becoming self-employed or starting my own business. During the summer of 1998, my good friend Butch told me he was quitting a part-time contract he had, teaching enterprise in our local post-primary schools. The position was there for me if I wanted it. Suddenly light bulbs starting to come on in my mind. Two days a week teaching enterprise and maybe another two days doing assessments. I had the bones of my own HR/career guidance business. It may seem a leap, but that's what I said about faith at the beginning of this. If I didn't know just what it was, I knew again, at that moment, that it was right to pursue.

The impetus grew, and the idea became an unmissable chance.

Within a very short period I found myself sitting in front of our CEO muttering the words:

'I'm leaving the company.'

Out of instinct, I handed back the corporate ladder and the company car keys.

They did everything they could to make me stay, and I really appreciated it. It was an extremely difficult decision, probably one of the most difficult I had ever to make. However, I did feel with opportunities like this life doesn't always give you a second chance. It was now or never, and I had to take it.

Armed with nothing other than a bundle of optimism and a cartload of courage I faced the fear and walked away from a corporate life for good. Nothing is everything. The future is certain only if you answer its call and follow it where it is leading.

Chapter 1 – Life Lessons

This is where I hope to lead you. Into your questions, quandaries and chances. It might be the best thing to ever happen to you. If you listen to me in the forthcoming chapters, you might also listen to yourself and fully utilise the potential you were born with, and which can change not just your career, but your entire life. Your combination lock needs time to twist, sequences will be tested, but it will spring open. You just need guidance.

Read on, and you will get it.

2

START FOLLOWING YOUR STAR

Chapter 2

Start Following your Star

I see career guidance as a lifelong process, needed at a number of very important stages in our life. Just as ancient mariners and explorers navigated journeys through following the stars, you have to pick yours and use tools for navigation. This is where guidance comes in. Career counselling on long journeys will often shorten your path to the work that suits your personal attributes and instincts.

The career adviser could best be described as the navigator who helps you steer the course. You are the one putting in the effort, hoisting the sails, who will make the passage through what comes. But, as the last chapter explains, most career consultants who are worth paying have worked hard at work and bear the scars and rewards of achievement. The best advice comes from those who have gone before you, who know the bigger picture you are trying to draw; you couple this advice with your own prevailing instinct. This is a conversation that ultimately will take miles, years, off your career journey.

Career guidance is for life, not just for the Christmas of your Leaving Cert year as it is viewed and used in this country. It has to be ongoing, as you will change so much over the course of your lifetime. The last chapter showed you I didn't even know what the right journey was for me until the opportunity presented itself to me twenty years into my working life. My reaction was to baulk, but my instinct prevailed, together with my willingness to look at possibilities and rise to the challenge.

The reality is that the career journey has gone from being one under sail to one on the *Starship Enterprise*. The perception of the careers consultant remains rooted in the seventies of the last century. It still hasn't caught up with the progress of the last fifty years.

Chapter 2 – Start Following Your Star

When people think of career guidance, they think of a careers teacher, showing them how to fill out CAO forms, giving help in selecting the ideal career that is going to serve us well for the rest of our lives. This is why it's an outdated image based on an outdated concept. Navigation has been changed forever by the Sat Nav and so has what people need from a careers consultant.

The model in peoples' minds might have worked in the sixties and seventies, where careers were much clearer cut if you received it. I didn't, and most people I know didn't receive it either. But if you did, the advice was straightforward. At that stage, with a Leaving Certificate, it would have been nursing/teaching for the girls, possibly banking/engineering for the boys.

The Civil Service or Semi-State bodies were other great fallbacks. Teenagers were thinking about pensions. If you were not school minded, or given the opportunity, as free education only arrived in the sixties, you looked for a trade. If you couldn't hold a hammer or sew a stitch, you turned to retail, hospitality or production lines. Maybe you helped on your farm.

Everywhere people sought work without thinking of the work's suitability in relation to them. This is how I ended up with the ammonia smell in my nostrils for four years – two in college and another two in a fertiliser factory.

The careers counsellor back then coached from the sideline of a narrow playing field of limited opportunities, governed by the need for a wage. However, this is no longer near adequate, due to the increasing complexity of the courses/qualifications /careers available to young people in this country.

The world has got smaller for navigators and larger for job seekers. It's no longer the sky as the limit; the new horizon is an entire universe. We are voyagers of enterprise pushing out into planetary explorations, two-thirds of future journeys are beyond what we already know exists in our solar system. Why?

Sixty-five percent of the employment opportunities our current school goers will seek and perform have not even been invented yet. And it is also apparent that they will not stick at one thing, but have the chance to change mind and course as they steer themselves through a working world undergoing a technical and social revolution. It is not inconceivable, and even good business sense, to learn Mandarin Chinese along with your business degree.

The modern emigrant might end up working in Beijing, where only thirty years ago it was more likely to be Boston or Birmingham.

We are advancing at such a rapid pace, it is widely accepted that people are going to have, as mentioned in the introduction, at least three different careers throughout their lifetime. So we as career consultants need to take clients where no one has gone before. More than ever we need to know ourselves within our employment because our employment is based on our ability to change and adapt.

Following is a brief overview of the stages and accompanying life transitions that career consultants commonly support people's work and interests in. Divided into age categories they all require different strategies, so I have come up with terms to describe them. You'll meet individual archetypes later, but these are the stages all kinds of individuals pass through, or avoid:

The 15 to 16ers - Transits –

Typically here, a student is studying for Junior Certificate or in Transition Year and is choosing subjects for Senior Cycle. The following scenario often repeats itself right across the country:

Lorna arrives home from school on Friday afternoon, with her list of subject choices, and tells her parents she has to pick choices the following week, that will affect the rest of her academic life. Lorna understands that she has to make choices for her fifth-year subjects. Her parents understand she has to make subject choices based on her predispositions. Together they work to make sense of what she is going to do. The feeling in most homes can be one of overwhelm. Also if her choices don't fall correctly, she will have to make compromises on the subjects she cares about and let some go. Bands of categories offer her little leniency. At least one subject she would have liked will not be a possibility. She will often have to make a choice based on which of her favourite subjects she does best in, rather than what she enjoys most of all.

A career at this point is at the far edges of her thinking, grades are her concern and keeping them up. Her parents see the bigger picture possibly, that grades are not all Lorna is about, but the option of getting her the perspective and help she needs is not on the table. What is on the table is dinner and a few other children to think of. A career consultant could make a world of difference even at this point, could point the seed of information that will flourish into a working life. Unfortunately little or no guidance is available at this stage.

Parents and children have to make the decisions on their own and often pay dearly for wrong choices.

The 17 to 18ers – Tacklers

There is a great secret hiding in plain sight in this age-group. They are advanced communicators technically and ill-prepared for course choices and work possibilities. They can tell you what's trending, but they don't know how to make core course choices for future work trends. Holding the whole world in their smartphones, in this era of technology, where careers are interstellar instead of on your doorstep, a black hole appears.

The truth of what it means not to be education and career guided in the Transit and Tackle stages becomes apparent. One-third of CAO applicants will vanish from sight by the time of their finals. Few parents ever hear colleges talking about the dropout rate on courses. It is not just a great secret but a great shame and stress. What follows are the consequences embodied in Lorna, who is going to illustrate the realities rarely addressed.

Lorna is now at Leaving Cert stage when she and all her year are making their CAO application. It arrives, like a document from another planet, offering a panoply of options. Some are in Donegal, others in Dublin. Where will she go? The family swim in a strong current of college and university open days together with CAO choices.

At this stage of picking courses, colleges and campuses, there are major implications. Lorna's parents thought she might need a few thousand, but education at third level is free. Isn't it? The bank account looks taxed. The future is not offering as much freedom as Lorna thought she would have. The parents are worried about how they will manage with her and her siblings all going to college over the next few years.

For parents without grant aid, who may be investing up to as much as €50,000 in their son's or daughter's education, this can be critically important and very stressful.

Non-Progression Scenario: Statistically we know now that one in six students who attend the first year of third level, will not progress on to do the second year. I estimate, from experience and what I research, that a further one in six will not complete second/third year.

Roughly speaking, one-third of students will not make the right choice. More about that later in terms of wider implications.

Lorna makes her choices based on limited information and is swayed by what her friends are doing as much as anything else, landing a college place in Dublin. First-year proves tough. Nobody had advised her prior to the application and enrollment process how difficult some of the modules she is studying would be. She does the best she can, but the range of subjects includes some she has no aptitude for.

She is struggling and sees the writing on the wall so, before her parents spend any more money on something she knows she can't finish, she de-registers from the course and is left devastated. Her parents have taken out a Credit Union education loan. She knows they're finding it hard so finds a job she doesn't want, to help pay it back. Life is disaffecting, and her morale sinks. It takes another couple of years for her to see her own big picture.

For students who don't progress, the results can be devastating, very damaging to one's self-esteem and confidence levels. Apart from this emotional cost, the financial cost to parents can be very significant, even prohibitive, as they face very steep tuition fees for repeat years.

Progression Scenario: What if Lorna carries on, feeling that this is the only option available to her? What if she struggles through the unfamiliar subjects? She is now part of the two-thirds who make it, finishing their education or apprenticeship.

We think that the situation is sorted for them, but is it? Not so based on my experience.

I see a high percentage of graduates needing career guidance following completion of their studies. Some of the main reasons for them needing consultation can be:

- Their primary degree did not turn out to be the degree they thought it was going to be.
- They have a nonspecific degree, and there are now no immediate prospects of getting a job without specialised study.
- They are now unsure their degree will lead them to the work that they thought it was going to provide them with.
- They have completed a degree in their area of interest, but it is one that needs a high degree of post-grad studies, such as psychology/ law and they do not want to or can't afford to continue with studies.

Lorna, who dragged herself over the line to become a graduate, comes to see me with a degree and a leaden heart because she doesn't want to use it. We look at lots of post-grad options, and her eyes light up a little. Then she sees one post-grad offering the option of work she was always interested in but never thought it was possible. A few hours consultation later and she is even considering voluntary work to build up her skills and CV.

There were options all along, but now she is making her own choices. She feels empowered because there is an endpoint. She wants to take out her own education loan. She'll get there. Just because someone listened, who could shed light and offer help.

The Late 20s – Testers

I meet a lot of adult clients at this stage in their lives. Up to this point, these people have been happy to exchange their work time for money, and this money is supporting quite a busy social life. There's a career clock as well as a biological one, and it starts to tick.

At this key age, people take stock. They have been working hard but haven't found the happiness in their career that they were seeking. Lorna in the progression scenario got sorted because she checked in with a careers consultant ten years previously.

But Joe, who focused on sport and the life that goes with it, who lived for weekends, now sees a fulfilled Monday to Friday as something worth investigating. It's at this age young adults seem to express their initial desire that they would like a career change and that the initial expectations they had about their career have not been met.

Someone like Joe might remember that he was good at a certain subject in school, or college, but with the lure of all the fun for a young man, he didn't put in the hours to turn it into an ambition. Now he wants to focus on who he is in his work, because he can see a time coming when he might have a family, or he's noticed someone at another desk who has been at it twenty years longer than him. There's a look on that face he doesn't want on his own.

He asks himself two questions:
- "How did I end up behind this desk?"
- "When am I going to do something to get away from it?"

He looks up Career Help in his search engine, finds my consultancy and does the online assessment. There, on screen, is what he once thought about doing. He makes a call.

The 30s – Trials

The thirties for a lot of working adults become the age of responsibility. At this time people are dealing with issues such as maternity leave and mortgages. Couples, in particular, are now working hard but probably not playing so hard. Every career move from now has to take the mortgage into consideration.

Joe and Lorna did something earlier, but Jane didn't. She held on because she thought she wanted to get a house before taking a new direction. She also met her partner or husband, and they wanted a family, so she decided to hang on for another few years since the maternity leave was good.

Her choices might be limited by a financial and familial obligation, but she still has options. One evening a week she might study for a starter qualification, or take up a part-time position to help her career prospects for what she really is.

This is where the word guidance needs to be heard in career consulting. If you are seeing someone who is making a career decision, you will hear and see who the person is. The guidance is not just about changing work; it is about changing a life.

The 40s – Thinkers

The next phase that people need support happens around the big 4-0. With the cards that arrive on the mantelpiece comes the thought:

I want to make the rest of my life into something.

People are becoming more aware of their work and the significant role that it plays in their life. I think at age 40 people are prepared to say they want a bit more from life. They begin to expect a little more meaning maybe. Sometimes, at this stage, they are prepared to make some sacrifices, maybe take a reduction in salary or work part-time in order to find work that is more purposeful.

Many begin thinking of working for themselves. People of this age and stage have gathered a lot of experience in the world and may now feel they want to go it alone and it;'s now or never. The prospect of self-employment doesn't seem as frightening as the prospect of never having tried it.

Lorna, Joe and Jane – one of them knows Paul and says he ought to get some help choosing his career. His wife agreed and bought him a present of a session. Paul took his fortieth birthday cards down from the mantelpiece and phoned the career guidance service. From the minute he walked in, he spoke about how much money he was making for his boss. From the minute he walked out, he began to work on his business plan.

With that plan in place, he broke the dream down into actions.

The 50 to 60 something's – Totallers

Not to be mistaken for teetotallers, at this stage I get clients who are becoming more philosophical about life, wanting to make a difference in other peoples' lives and in the world. They want to take a little time for themselves.

They are seeing the total picture and are breaking out the champagne for having made it through the rigours and demands of the decades behind them. They feel they have worked all these years and now they actually deserve something a little easier. Life slows, and it also deepens to have more meaning. This may also be the beginning of the empty nester phase, where parents have put children through college, and they can be more flexible now around income and salaries.

Then there's the R word. Retirement! It's not always the golden event people envisage. The lump sum and the lack of routine might be a dream for some, but for others, it is worrying. Career help might seem a misnomer at this stage, but people who may be ready to retire from paid employment may not be finished contributing to the community. So many people at this stage need support.

Therese has seen Paul flying in his new business, and she asks him how did he get the courage to quit in his late forties and take a risk? She reveals she would love to. He advises her to book someone like me and tells the story of how one session changed his life.

'I'm leaving work, not looking for it.' She sounds uncertain.

'But work isn't leaving you.' He smiles at her.

'That's true. I don't want to do nothing all day.' She takes down the number.

She doesn't call straight away but gets around to it when she's ready to do more than being at home. In her session, she talks about her work and all she ever hoped for on the way was a raise. Now, after three months at home, she'd be happy to work for nothing. I have very good news for her. Voluntary groups need her expertise. She may be retiring now but she is far from finished, and she needs to know what she is going to do for the rest of her life.

Her role, administrating a new charity, becomes the most meaningful one she ever had. There is a new course to steer.

As a team – the guide navigating, the career client sailing – we have covered the lifespan of work. The training, initiation, promotion advancement and retirement process were a circumnavigation. All the work becomes an experience, and this is used to help others and in turn ourselves. The key stages were keys in the locks of life, described in the last chapter, but they were all because people were experiencing confusion. The journey itself is what happens when we have the courage to leave port and take our own course.

If I saw all the Lorna's, aged 15, in time, I wonder how many Paul's would have to come through my door? Hopefully more! It is never ever too late. Work is how we live, but if you're honest with yourself and willing to take time and stock to think about it, you will find yourself doing more than you ever imagined possible.

Figure 1 – Life Stages

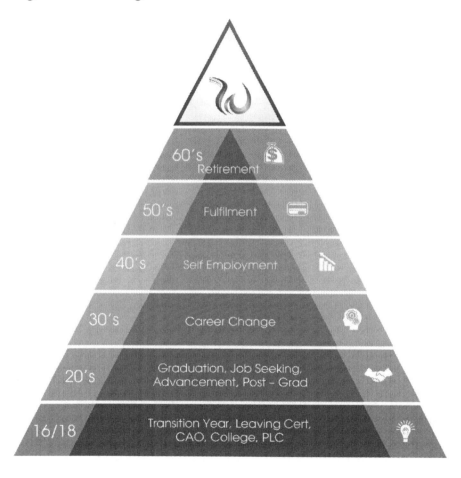

Career guidance is not just for Leaving Certificate, it is for life, (See Fig. 1) and people are making career choices from 16

right up to 70 plus, now that retirement ages are pushing up and people are more active after work. At each stage, a level of advice and support is needed. The guidance process should be providing this support from the incubus to the outcome.

In Ireland, we seem to think that if a Leaving Cert student receives a fifteen-minute career interview that they are sorted for life. Of course, this is a complete illusion.

What we need is a process where people can avail of guidance from experienced advisors, at all stages throughout their working life.

A Hidden Catastrophe

The stages part of this chapter focused on the great secret. Well, now I am naming it by something else – because it is also a catastrophe, of esteem, of resources within a family and within a government.

Career guidance does not belong in schools because the only people who work in schools are teachers and supporting staff. The bank clerks, investors, nurses, doctors, shop assistants, business owners, builders, and accountants are all outside this institution, working in what is the real world. Unfunded by State, relying on acumen and productivity levels to stay afloat and/or employed.

This is not a criticism of guidance counsellors or teachers in second level schools. Most have a strong desire and motivation to help and guide young students. However, to work in secondary schools, you must hold a secondary teaching qualification which is now a two-year full-time master's degree (the old H-dip).

This effectively excludes all those from a non-teaching background from working as a guidance counsellor, including those with valuable life and work experience. Guidance counsellors are doing the best they can with limited resources, especially the most important resource which is time. In addition, because they work in the school system, they are on holidays in August when the real need arises!

Career guidance is now often taught as a classroom subject and for a number of reasons it just doesn't work. Guidance Counsellors now also have to teach their core subject in classes, and very often they are unable to give badly needed one to one career guidance. The school year does not suit the needs of school leavers for whom August is a vital month, offering CAO decisions and opportunities.

The result is the hidden catastrophe for government, community and family.

There is an illusion that all this career planning is being sorted in school hours. A career guidance system is completely different to a school system and doesn't belong in it at all. It is a vital component of a working life, but it still hasn't left the classroom, in the Irish impression of it. In the UK it's available on the High Street, through Government agencies, to all ages. Like most things in this book, I will name it, but I will also show it.

Dragon's Den - for all Ages

No wonder the Welsh have a dragon on their flag. This wonderful, reactive, proactive country have seen that career choices are life choices and they have put government where that need is. Career Choices Dewis Gyrfa Ltd (CCDG) is a wholly owned subsidiary of the Welsh Government which was formed on 1 April 2013. Trading as *Gyrfa Cymru Careers Wales,* they provide what the previous section addresses: All age, independent and impartial careers information and advice.

There are dragon's dens up and down the country. If you're 19 or 99, you can make an appointment. The overall focus for their service is to help people make effective decisions and become independent in managing their careers. The younger ones are given a measure of realism while the older ones are given a measure of optimism or the other way around since everyone is different.

The work of *Careers Wales* includes making realistic career decisions and plans and ensuring successful progression and positive outcomes for individuals, who they support to gain appropriate training, further learning or employment. *Careers Wales* helps to develop the nation's skills base and to support the effectiveness of expenditure on education and training. So it doesn't just boost individuals. It is contributing to the economic and social well-being of the country. It's probably even assisting the rugby team to take back the Championship from their tormentors.

This is what they say about themselves:

Career Choices Dewis Gyrfa Ltd (CCDG): Why do we exist?

Career decisions are among the most important decisions people make throughout their lives and careers information, advice and guidance can help to:

- Improve knowledge and awareness of learning opportunities and the labour market.
- Improve self-awareness, raise individual aspirations and support people to make effective decisions about their careers.
- Increase access to, and completion of, learning and training.
- Motivate people to **manage their careers**, improve application and interview skills and be resilient in adapting their plans when circumstances change.
- Address inequality by focusing on the needs of groups who are under-represented in employment, learning or training and by challenging stereotyping.

Saving Personal Esteem Saves Society Money

CCDG is not just saving the confidence of working people. It is saving the government money in poorly made career choices. If the careers dragon's dens were available in Ireland the following might not occur:

Approximately 6,200 Irish school leavers would not drop out of their chosen third level programme, at a cost, let me repeat the figure because it's worth remembering; it is estimated to be greater than €35 million.

They simply have no one qualified to talk to, so they do what they have been trained by our school system to do, they accept what is offered without question.

- If your car breaks down, you get a mechanic.
- If your body breaks down, you get a doctor.
- If your career breaks down, only three percent will see a trained careers consultant.

Life exposure leads to new choices and challenges. So you need a trained professional to advise you, who has been there and done that bit. And what of the parents who are saving to make board and tuition fees for a first-degree sitter? They have the illusion that once their son or daughter lands in UCD or any other Colege or University, they are sorted. But most aren't ready.

Not because they couldn't, they have not been prepared properly to make a choice.

What to do? Let's Talk Work before We Get Work

If I got into Government I would set up a semi-state governing body over career choices, like the Education and Training Board, or the Enterprise Board, but exclusively for careers. I would give school leavers, all 60,000 of them, regular appointments to guide them through choices and possibilities. Apart from school hour appointments, which should form part of the curriculum, the service would be outside of school hours, at evenings and weekends, throughout the holidays, when all the decisions are actually taken. Why? Because career guidance is a separate entity – it covers adults and students and is an ongoing process, not a one-off.

Career guidance for school leavers should be an eight-hour affair; a working day spread over two to three sessions. Even in my private practice, this is offered in slots of four hours, in packages designed to suit the parents' pockets.

Career Guidance is Not Child-Friendly – but Adult Vital

When my phone rings and an adult is on the end, they will often make apologies as they think it's just for school-age clients.

41

Career guidance is an acceptable phrase, but it isn't an appropriate one. The existing model falls short of what is deserved.

Career guidance should be for all not just the wealthy. Three percent of school leavers will use my service. The comparative cost is huge, as the work is ongoing not a one-off. The navigational needs of our working population are not being served by long-term disinterest. School choices are not short term; they are the first domino. To set a course, you need to consult. The journey shortens, your finances stabilise, your relationships benefit.

You become who you were meant to be. You see a career crisis as an opportunity. Each wrong decision a learning curve if it makes us wiser and we are on the right path.

Sometimes we don't know what we are truly capable of and it takes the witness of guidance to foster the belief that may not be there.

The Irish employment situation thirty years ago was if you were lucky you had a job. This created a sense of privilege in people just to be paid, even if it was work they were not suited to and had little interest in. Michelle came for a session having already slipped under the portcullis of unemployment and was inside the castle of the regular wage earner, putting in hours and time in exchange for money. But her authentic self was lying outside this remit - back out, over the moat, into the unknown forest of - *what do I truly want?*

JFK once alluded to the fact that the Chinese character for *crisis* is a merging of the characters of *danger* and *opportunity*. The truth is a little more complex than this, but the ethos is the same. If we are safely paid and able to handle the employment we have, there is no real reason to change, but if we are acutely dissatisfied, we are being offered the motivation to make more of and with our lives. We just have to go through the agony of indecision, of searching, to find our possibility. Then we have to be brave enough to make our way towards our true purpose.

Michelle arrived in the office having completed a computer/administration course with the then FAS, after which she gained employment with a local company.

'This company was in the early stages of development, and I felt fortunate to gain employment as many who completed the course didn't have this opportunity.'

The initial relief to have found work locally, in a firm that was starting up when many were closing down, soon materialised into awareness that, much as she was good at it, the role was not for her:

'My role in the company was pretty basic admin work and really not very inspiring. With years my responsibility grew.'

Given her admirable skill set, she started to take on more than the job requirements, pushing for more responsibility and proving her worth, including putting in overtime without any gain other than seeing the company blossom.

'As a result, with company mergers and takeovers, I gained more responsibility moving from a very junior to a management position. My income grew significantly, and this had a big impact.' The honey trap was set. 'I made my decision to stay with this company.'

Like all wasps will tell you, honey is not worth giving up your flight for. The pressure she took on readily in the first instance began to wear her down, and the company methods were not a good match for her own moral compass. The money was good but did not come stress-free. You could sink in the prospects, and the beginning of Michelle's crisis began. Her true north was pulling her, the magnetising of her bigger prospects forcing her into the questions around her wage packet and the consequences of receiving it each month:

'I wasn't happy in the job, or with some of the people I worked with. There was enormous pressure to reach the monthly individual, group and branch targets. Some of the business transactions of the company I found hard to deal with as to me they seemed unethical and dishonest. I will admit to closing my eyes to this for some time and storing it in my subconscious. I could use fear as an excuse but it wasn't long before my conscience kicked in and I began to question myself'.

The days wore on, but her work ethic and desire to remain employed gave her cause to swallow antacids for the indigestion of watching things she would rather not have seen and hearing things she would rather not have heard.

'There was so much company politics, nepotism and favouritism within the company walls, I felt emotionally, mentally and physically drained from negotiating it all. So much so that I couldn't give anything to anyone in my personal life.'

Regardless of how much we detach from the work environment, if it isn't right for us in the long run, it will impede all other areas. Michelle, having been there from the beginning, could not but challenge some of the events in the business and the people they were affecting. As the company grew, her work in helping it to do so became disregarded. She became one of the affected. Mergers brought in more of the values she was resisting. There was a growing disregard for what she had put in.

'As one who was there at the start of the company, who had much to do with building it from the ground to a very successful business, I felt I wasn't treated well. My potential wasn't being used when the companies merged. To be honest, I felt used and betrayed by my former employer.'

Added to this that her employer still wished to act as if they felt the same concern for the stalwart they were not supporting. When in Rome, do as Romans do, or move to a different city:

'I felt stuck and stagnating. While some of my colleagues were decent people, there was always an undercurrent of pressure, need to impress, or indeed behave, in a manner that wasn't natural to me.'

The money kept coming. But the consternation was growing, and powerful forces were at play.

'With a mortgage to pay and a feeling of inadequacy, I pushed on in this job for some years. I will be the first to admit it was all about the money. I couldn't put my finger on where this feeling of inadequacy manifested from. I had lots of tacit knowledge of the industry, and I performed in my job always giving one hundred percent, getting results and taking ownership.'

But Michelle was a lot more besides, and the internal feelings were fracturing the façade:

'On the outside, I appeared as a true suit wearing, decision-making, high-powered professional. On the inside, I was consumed with boredom, and a feeling of there has to more to life than this constant feeling of inadequacy, target reaching, constant refereeing of internal disputes and office dramas, while at the same time underutilising the many skills I felt I had'.

'Looking back I do feel I was on the verge of a breakdown and thankfully due to the love and support from my husband this never manifested.'

The breakdown is often the point of breakthrough. Michelle could not contain her crisis. She had to look for methods and motives for change. Enter Seamus Whitney.

'By chance, I saw in the local newspaper details of a course being held in local Enterprise Centre. It was specifically designed for people who were in long-term employment and felt they needed to upskill. *Oh my God*, I thought, *are they talking about me*? So with no hesitation, I applied. Having been out of education for some time, it was safe to say I felt anxious but excited. Being the person who gives a hundred percent to any endeavour, I applied the same here. On reflection what it did for me was made me realise there were lots of people in similar work situations. I had potential and options. I had to decide to make the change, as no one else had the power to do this for me. It gave me the confidence to explore these options, with support from Seamus and other participants'.

'The course had a big impact on me. I distinctly remember saying during one exercise that I wanted to do what Seamus was doing. It's a funny thing now, but when I reflect on that course, I realised that up to that point I had never received any structured career guidance in my life. I wasn't even aware that such a thing as career guidance even existed.'

It gave her the future focus that her existing position could not allow. While it demanded a lot of her, she set to work, using her key traits of focus, willingness and hard work.

'It took many steps for me to accomplish this and while trying to figure out my path, I completed studies in psychology, adult training and development, accountancy and business. Delving into courses, taking guidance and advice, trying to make a decision, wanting to get it right. Weighing up all the pros and cons.'

Change however is never straightforward. Michelle had to endure the uncertainties and daily reconfiguration of priorities that were now changing her life. In place of the agony she had experienced in suppressing her instinct, she now had to follow it.

Looking back, she sees:

'A very confusing time, mixed emotions, balancing financial responsibility with emotional needs. Not being able to see the light for the trees and all the time my husband saying: "Do what makes you happy."'

The honey trap is hard to release from. But then providence conspired, bringing on yet another crisis which upended her dogged, determined progress and forced her to bring the future she wanted closer and more quickly than she might have done. It also offered her a healthy dollop of unfairness to make the medicine even harder to take:

'Decision time was made for me when I was made redundant. Others who did very little for the company remained securely employed. As I mentioned, I already felt used by company mergers and the politics that went around them.' And she saw that the future was here. 'After this observation I closed the door on that part of my life, distancing myself from previous colleagues and not getting involved in any of their stories of despair. It felt like a big weight was lifted. Yes, I was concerned about impending financial strain, but I was determined to use this as an opportunity, rather than let it bring me down'.

'With much encouragement, in the form of straight talking and advice from Seamus, and my husband's kind encouragement and belief in me, I began delving into the possibility of doing more courses and made the decision to re-enter education. I remember Seamus asking me what I would feel walking up to the stage to receive my Third Level scroll. The decision was made.

'Having studied and enjoyed psychology, and adult training and development, I felt that indeed I want to work with people in the area of development and education. College, training and up-skilling, the things that helped me were what I wanted to help people with myself. I had been through it, and I was good at it, as I continue to be. I am happy now I am working with people in the area of education, in a role that I enjoy.'

The road less travelled is now taken, and Michelle sees the benefits, if not in immediate income, in the response of clients to her work and the growth of that client base which will lead in time to more prospects and financial reward for work she loves rather than hates. Her reputation grows with each client encounter, and the word of mouth feedback on her approach and ability is outstanding. Many come to her because they have heard from the last person who sat in the chair beside her. Added to this she is her own boss, so her work practice now aligns with her values and beliefs.

'While I may not see the same financial rewards as in my previous life, I do see a more emotionally fulfilling and mentally stimulating reward. I am proud to say that I am now self-employed and, while this brings its own challenges, I am enjoying it. I see a future where I am in control of my life to the degree that one can be in control.'

We all have things to accept, but in the right position there is so much to hope for:

'I feel my potential is endless; I am supported and work in an environment where I am appreciated and part of society. My feeling of inadequacy is gone. The simple answer to my own question of why I was feeling inadequate in my previous job, is that I was working like a robot to earn a buck with no emotional connection to my life.

'With education, reflection and real people, I have blossomed into my authentic existence. Could I have done it without proper guidance and support from someone like Seamus? I really don't think so. To make real change, we need a person to take an interest in us and nurture us on the path. I'm forever grateful to Seamus for being that person for me.'

3
MECHANISMS AND MIRACLES

Chapter 3

Mechanism and Miracles

Matching Interests to Potential

'To be yourself in a world that is constantly trying to make you something else is the greatest accomplishment'
Ralph Waldo Emerson

 As you have read, I spent my college years and subsequent decades doing first a course, then jobs I was not suited to, but doing them very well. The standards I reached sublimating my preference and using my instinct to perform to a high standard or not at all, promoted me into my true interest. So I know the reality of being a square peg in a round hole.

Today going through the college and work process without self-knowledge is not the norm. We have come some way to seeing the more we know ourselves, the better we will do in work aligned to our interests. But that is us as individuals. In assessing our working future, we need assistance. The seeds of this must be sown at senior secondary school. But no one is thinking sufficiently of the medium to long-term gain. I have heard so many parents say this to students unhappy at third level:

'Stick with it. At least you will be qualified for something.'

So they begin to make themselves into the kind of square peg that will fit. There is so much to be said of this in terms of emotional and social fallout, but that is not for this chapter. We will come to it, as it has to be addressed. What we are about here is looking at the mechanisms that poorly serve the miracle of a human being who is full of potential to do a job that works for them well, which in turn works for our society.

Had these miracles in action had the right advice at senior cycle they might have ended up on the course most suitable for them. A core issue of this book centres on how much emphasis is put on the school/college/work organisation's methods of assessing your predisposition to the course or career you have applied to do. You are tested more than interviewed, and this is where the first ball is dropped. As a careers advisor, one of the most common questions I get asked is:

'Do you do aptitude tests?'

The answer is yes, but what I would like to say upfront is this. While aptitude tests can play a role in determining what career suits a candidate, they are far from complete and do not give anything like the full picture. Indeed for some areas like nursing – aptitude tests tell us very little about the person's suitability. In careers such as in social work, personality profiling would probably be more important. But it is still not everything.

In the seventies, Dana won the Eurovision with a song called *All Kinds of Everything*. It's the perfect title for what an aptitude test does. It offers a prospective employer, or educator, a general assessment of the group who have applied to them, all kinds of information, but nothing truly specific. They will show who is good at tests primarily, rather than the individual who has a strong aptitude. They suggest rather than predict potential.

Why?

Tests provide insights of the certain abilities; interviews offer a fully embodied impression of a person, their values and instincts. No score will select a candidate, but the response at interview will validate what the score showed. There are so many variables that cannot be gauged without human response. An experienced interviewer/educator will know the kind of person who will fit into the scenarios they are already part of. The intangibles are often as vital to a working and learning environment as the tangibles, as they are strong indicators of true intelligence and performance.

Sometimes I feel parents in particular, who are more familiar with old style IQ tests, think that there is security in aptitude tests and the results. If a person scores sufficiently high on an aptitude test, well then that should determine the direction for the rest of their life. However, as I will point out, that is far from correct.

First and foremost – work pressures and exam pressures, while both can be pressure, they are different kinds. A person who performs brilliantly in exams might find the engagement with others in a working environment hard to cope with. A person who performs at work might underachieve in exam terms. So an aptitude test excelled shows someone who can excel at aptitude testing!

An aptitude test is on any given day a screenshot of a person. It does not take into account the full extent of their:

- Passion and Insight
- Persistence and Initiative
- Personality and Ideas

An employer or educator going purely on a test result is similar to an egg sorter. They are looking at a product – placing it in a niche in a box – then moving on to the next package on the production line. It is using an indicator and leaving out instinct. An employer who does this alone goes out of business. As for the educator doing so –well it happens, and it is endemic, and it is proved by the vast dropout rate on third level courses. The great secret that everyone knows - this issue meriting the attention it is not receiving.

The human personality and individual predisposition is not a factor in the filtering of most third level candidates. The combination of tests done by some organisations will look at the results, and give them parity with the interview process, meaning they most likely will not let the candidate who had a right instinct for the course slip through their fingers. We will come to DAT in a minute! When you are sifting through potential candidates, you use a combination of indicators and instinct. Human contact is vital, as a person's vitality is half their suitability along with their training and aptitude.

Mechanisms and Miracles

What are aptitude tests? Simply put they are mechanisms for measuring the aptitude, in a brief time span, of an eternal miracle – the human being. So they are a tool but not an entirety. The modern term for aptitude tests is "psychometric" (measurement for the mind). There are a number of different types of psychometric tests available:

Interest Inventory – this is not really an aptitude test, but it is a very important questionnaire in helping to tease out a candidate's interests. There are no right or wrong answers to an Interest Inventory. A person just answers like or dislike, yes or no, depending on the work situation presented to them.

Aptitude Tests – these ability tests measure candidate's ability levels on a number of scales, the most common of these would be numeric and verbal abilities. These are often used as entrance tests, for example, entry into An Garda Síochána or Public Service Administration type jobs.

Personality Tests – these tests measure a person's personality traits on a range of different indicators. Popular personality tests include Myers Briggs, Personality Profiler and the 16 PF5 Personality Profiler. Personality Tests are often used by the recruiters, by trying to establish the type of person they may be taking on into their company. They are also widely used in the area of personal or self-development and are known to give clients or candidates in-depth analysis of themselves and their personality traits.

In my experience, psychometric tests can play a role but only form one part of the bigger picture. Why? I have lived and worked with people and their personalities for sixty years. I have worked with people and their personalities in relation to careers for half that time span. I have never yet met one person who was the same as another.

The Individual and the Assessment Procedure

Assessing a group with one test will never present the entirety. The fact that paid websites exist for psychometric testing is an indicator that there is a system to circumvent here. Tests are easy once you know how to do them and this can come from practice. You can improve performance by practising on various websites.

Structured tests give a structured interpretation. Results do not take into account the:

- The anxiety level of the test sitter.
- Sitter's errors of interpretation of some questions.
- Assessor's ability to read sitter's handwriting.
- Assessor's error of interpretation of some answers.
- Errors in the framework of the test apparatus.

The second last point applies when a firm buys in tests, but not markers of those tests. A person who is not trained in assessing the answers will be more likely than someone who has been, to make an error.

The last point applies very much to the use of DATS tests– a blanket response offering the blankest, thinnest response, to the Tower of Babel that is the Leaving Certificate year cohort.

DATS Spelling Disaster

DATS, Differential Aptitude Tests, are a cheap alternative to an expensive problem.

Used widely by the Department of Education in the school education system, they are normally given at Junior Cert or Transition Year and supposedly help students choose subjects for the senior cycle. In my experience, DATS tests do far from that. To my knowledge, they are very confusing and often leave students clueless about what they are actually saying. In some cases, they can conflict student's core abilities, and this can lead to stress and anxiety. The very thing they are supposed to highlight they mask in those cases.

Being nervous and/or confused plays a major factor in your test results. DATS bring together both obstacles. The results are often chance and rarely incisive. If it's broken why bother fixing it? It is a system already in place. If it's already in place why is it allowed to remain when it's broken? The results often alleviate parental anxiety over their loved child's future. Very often parents attend an assessment with us and proudly produce this sheet of detailed DATS tests. Very few really have any idea as to what the test results are saying.

DATS has four letters in common with the word DisAsTrouS, that would be my overall opinion of these over-rated tools. The best strategy for their use, in my view, would be to scrap them completely and own up to the fact that they are not serving interests of the takers or the parents. They are just a mass-produced alternative to providing the individualised information and guidance young people need at this stage of their education.

The expense a parent goes through, the esteem a young person loses in choosing the wrong course and using their parents' savings, in finding they went through school to end up on a path that is not right, the loss of government funds in funding unsuitable courses, would be put paid to by investing in properly funded career and course advice.

Sure they might show what you might be good at, but do they show you what you are truly interested in and potentially passionate about? Just because you're good at it, doesn't mean you want to do it. How did I realise this? By helping parents and young people who had come because there was a need for it. Their DATS test said one thing, but their mouths another. They were trying the wrong digits in their combination, lulled by the praise of a computer generated result.

Then there are the people who aren't made to feel proud at all, whose school record shows problems, when they sit in front of me I see nothing but a potential that a system has failed to notice because the parameters were too general and the learner was lost. Read on.

Testing for Specific Learning Difficulties.

Specific learning difficulties, dyslexia in particular, often needs an educational psychology assessment, carried out by a qualified professional such as an educational psychologist. Sometimes a student may qualify assessment through their school via the Department of Education, but waiting lists can be long. Some parents take their children to a private educational psychologist and pay.

The test is very comprehensive, and normally assesses students using the Wechsler Intelligence Scale for children. It comprises of four indices measuring verbal comprehension, perceptual reasoning, working memory and processing speed. The report often runs through five or six pages and is quite detailed but again often requires further interpretation for parents and students who sometimes find it difficult to understand the percentile scales used.

What is probably most important within the report is the recommendation sheet that follows, which normally gives the student a series of exercises, designed to improve the specific learning problem that they have.

Very often, these recommendations are used by the school to gain certain measures and resources from the Department of Education for the student. They are also often used to supplement DARE (Disability Access Route to Education) applications within the CAO and can qualify students for support such as a reader, or a spelling waiver, for the state exams.

Following my training in the area of aptitude testing, I quickly began to use these tests with my clients. I remember Saturday morning sessions in my local Credit Union, taking a group of young people and running a whole battery of tests on them.

Later, when I had the scores, I would meet with them individually and give them information on scores they had attained in verbal comprehension, or their ability in the area of diagrammatic reasoning. What I found was that although I was giving students information on areas of strength and weakness, they weren't really that interested in those results.

Sometimes a student would have a very good aptitude in the area of numeric ability for example, but they would tell me flatly that they had no interest in working with numbers, or that they hated accounting and had no intention of studying any type of business courses.

In another situation, a student might have a good ability for engineering, but maths might have been weak. The student would have no intention of taking a course with the high degree of mathematics. In a lot of cases, the students would say something like:

'Fine, I have good aptitudes, but I just don't want to work in those areas.'

In a lot of cases, they just wanted to talk, to ask questions that should have been answered by the time they sat with me. They wanted to address, not just aptitude, but personhood. The relationship and prospective questions came thick and fast:

'What is the work actually like that I'm going for?'
'How long will I be studying for to get the job I want?'
'What would I be doing before I can get to do what I want?'
'How much would I be earning? '
'Where can I go to learn all this exactly?'

They seemed much more interested in how to qualify, where the best courses were, what subjects they might be studying in which college, than reviewing aptitude test results. But for the fifteen minutes of fame that a Leaving Cert student may get with a career guidance teacher, that teacher may have the DATS assessment in front of them. These students may still be pointed in the exact direction they told me on Saturday in the Credit Union they didn't want to go into:

'You're getting an A in accounting Johnny.'
'But I hate being at a desk.'

The career guidance counsellor under pressure now to teach as well as consult on a one to one, can look like they aren't even considering the student. The student thinks the CGT is no use at their job, a thing I often hear, but in fact, they have no opportunity to be good at it because of state made decisions on funding, teaching and timetable. Grades come into it, of course, but the biggest factor of all is motivation.

One session, given in Leaving Cert year, is a broad-based antibiotic. You might wipe out the problem, but you're taking a lot of other things down at the same time.

Students Need Time to Make Lifetime Choices

So, when assessing a student's suitability for a particular career, it's important to take all aspects pertaining to that student into account. In addition to looking at their attitudes and aptitudes, it's obviously very important to look at their CAO points.

The more important thing is to take into account the subjects they are studying, whether at Higher or Ordinary level, and the grades that they can realistically achieve in those subjects. It's only at this stage that we mix these indicators with their interests in particular careers. This is so important in terms of assessing a student.

Sitting down, looking at all the indicators and most importantly, I think, creating a safe space for the client to discuss their fears and to ask questions. This is the big benefit of holding one to one career guidance advice sessions.

Most inventions happen because an individual seeks out a service and it doesn't exist. So I came up with a solution in a space where there should have been one, considering it is dealing with the lives, hopes and expectations of all our futures – our next generation - our young people.

I needed it so much; I invented the tool.

There was an advertisement on TV for shavers at one time. The CEO said he liked the product so much he bought the company. I needed my own service so much, to plug this gap, I came up with it. Over a period of ten years to help me establish what motivated each client, I began to develop my own methods for assessing: a series of questionnaires and scenarios, which I designed to tease out each client's preferences for selected career areas.

When I had assimilated six specialist areas, I combined these into one comprehensive online assessment tool: *Soon to Be Me*™.

I tested these methods over a further two to three years until I was happy that they give me a true and accurate reflection of each person's career preferences. I will not attempt to assess any client now without them completing this assessment prior to each session or consultation with me.

It's never too late to pick up the learning. While I am referring to the young people I assess, the model works with all ages. *Soon to Be Me*™ is now available online to all who wish to use it for themselves. Probably the best way to understand it is to experience it. Send an email to info@whitneycareerguidance.com to receive a discounted code for your *Soon to Be Me* ™ assessment. See what it tells you about your preferences.

At a recent coaching seminar, *Mindstream* owner Sean Farrell, one of Ireland's leading coaches, defined coaching as: 'Deep listening combined with brilliant questions.'

Coaching and career guidance is not about telling people what to do, but facilitating a process where people can tap into the answers contained deep inside them. I believe our main role as career advisors is to do exactly that. First, we must earn the trust and respect of each of our clients. Then, in building this relationship, we allow our clients to safely explore their career preferences and discern what suits them best in terms of their interests and abilities. Then we look at their capacity to complete the necessary steps towards qualifications. The single most important factor for successful assessment is time.

Students need to be listened to by a good listener who can hear their concerns and allay their fears. There are thousands of books, prospectuses and web pages available, but they only seem to confuse the students and adults even more.

No One Formula, No One Fix, Just Soon to be You

There is no one formula fits all. If a client's career preferences haven't quite surfaced as yet, there is no quick fix to make this process happen more quickly. As a matter of fact, this is likely to be counterproductive, especially if the client happens to drop out of a course that is not suitable. I know I am saying it a lot since the first chapter and I will be saying it in the last chapter. I cannot say it enough. Here lies one of the biggest problems with the way career guidance is currently managed in schools. Like everything else it is based on a faulty assumption that every seventeen to eighteen year old falls within the average criteria, coupled with the clarity they need on what career to choose for the rest of their life.

What an illusion this is, it would be funny except for the hidden and sometimes calamitous consequences that result. A third of learners at third level, falling out of courses they should never have taken.

Their fall affects their:

- Futures
- Finances
- Focus
- Fulfilment

All compromised because they could not gain the valuable hours of consultation to find their clarity. Aside from these F-factors, there are also parents coping with the fears they have of the fundamentals. They have raised a child in a world that underwent a working revolution. Not unlike the scythe labourer watching their offspring seek employment in the new 'satanic mills' of the industrial revolution, today's twenty-first-century parent, has to witness, consult and assist their smartphone progeny.

How will their son or daughter take their place in a world, they as workers never even contemplated? A world of high-speed technology and light speed change? A world where the state guidance system for school leavers still employs antiquated attitudes and practices for assessment? Put simply. They can't. The right help is required urgently.

DisAsTer can lead to catastrophe. We need proper mechanisms of assessment, engagement and interview, to determine the miraculous potential of each new adult.

4

MAKING THE INVISIBLE VISIBLE

Chapter 4

Making the Invisible Visible

Choosing Your Career Archetypes

'No one was born into the world whose work is not born with him.'
James Russell Lowell, 1891–91

For two decades I have done what Sean Farrell defined coaching as. I have listened deeply and have heard what clients are not saying, as much as what they state. Often it is in the gaps between responses that I find the place where I can see the potential arising. Confidence may prevent a client from setting too high a goal, but that is where a good career consultation comes in.

Clients begin to hear themselves and, with prompting, to believe in themselves and possibilities in a few short hours. How? Firstly if they book to see me, they are ready for change or have to. But, once they are working on the issues, how can a lifetime pattern be adjusted within the parameters of a consultation?

Understanding is everything and each individual might be alone in what they are going through but never alone in how they think. In fact, there are many others who will be similar to them, and despite the fact we are all unique we tend to belong to certain tribes where careers are concerned. These tribes are archetypes (See Fig. 3) – traits that groups of individual's share that give them commonality which they then express in their own unique way.

During the past twenty years of working closely with clients, I have recognised specific behavioural patterns and personality traits that seem to repeat time and time again in my practice. This collection of attitudes, values and preferences is harder to describe and cannot be measured using traditional psychometric aptitude or IQ tests.

They are innate dispositions that often are not acknowledged in straightforward assessment. The best term I can use to describe these patterns is that they are archetypal. The term *archetype* has its origins in ancient Greek. The root words are *archein,* which means *original* or *old*; and *typos,* which means *pattern, model* or *type.* The combined meaning is 'an original pattern' of which all other similar persons, objects, or concepts are derived, copied, modelled, or emulated. Of course, the concept of archetypes is not new. They form part of the bedrock of Swiss psychiatrist and psychoanalyst, Carl Gustav Jung's, theory of the human psyche. The founding father of analytical psychology believed that universal, mythic characters reside within the collective unconscious of people the world over.

Archetypes represent fundamental human motifs of our experience as we evolved. They are our inherited ancestral potential and the process of living, the choices we make, the experiences we have, bring about our destiny. We are born with potential but do we reach it? This is the human quandary and quest.

Consequently, archetypal influences evoke deep emotions, often beyond the reach of everyday understanding. They are the impetus which if we observe and act on, will bring about changes and a full sense of self.

Although there are many archetypes, Jung defined twelve primary ones that symbolize basic human motivations. Each type has its own set of values, meanings and personality traits. Some types share a common driving source, for example, types within the ego set are driven to fulfil ego-defined agendas.

Most, if not all people, have several archetypes at play in their personality construct. However, one tends to preside over the multiplicities of the general personality. The same can be said for the patterns within people that I see on a regular basis. When advising people regarding career development, it is helpful to know which archetypes are at play in order to gain personal insight into behaviours and motivations.

Multiple Intelligences – the Prism of Human Potential

A prism can be used to break up light into its constituent colours – the ones we see in rainbows. We tend, though there are exceptions, to have a presiding archetype that governs our instinct, with feedback from others forming our psyche. So we are capable of working and thinking, in a number of different ways. This flexibility, this adaptability, helped us rise through the ranks to the top of the food chain.

There is more than one way of thinking, and we often employ different methods, while some will be stronger in us than others. Our intellect evolved over millions of years, so it is capable of a lot more than sitting a successful Leaving Certificate. It is a honed, refined, sophisticated tool and our greatest gift.

How we learn can often indicate who we are and just what we are capable of.

The developmental psychologist Howard Gardner developed a theory of multiple intelligences that help in understanding the emergence of career based archetypes. Gardner's multiple intelligences formed out of his own experience. He had a wish as a father which he expressed publicly:

'I want my children to understand the world, but not just because the world is fascinating and the human mind is curious. I want them to understand it so that they will be positioned to make it a better place.'

He, in turn, did this not just for his children but for all learners.

The same impetus that makes a parent send a child to me also makes an adult want to follow a latent career instinct – the desire to learn more about themselves and to work in the way most suited. It made Howard Gardner view intelligence in all its forms and named what we had lost sight of in education. In short, he had a hunch that we were corralling learning into narrow rote, rather than letting it be discovered through instinctive approaches. That was his potential; he reached it through blood, sweat, tears and documentation, endless research and compiling of data and interviews.

His theory emerged and: 'Documents the extent to which students possess different kinds of minds and therefore learn, remember, perform, and understand in different ways.' The world can be known through many approaches. Language, logical-mathematical analysis, spatial representation, musical thinking, the use of the body to solve problems or to make things, an understanding of other individuals, and an understanding of ourselves, are just some of them.

Gardner has defined more and is considering more since his definitive book *Frames of Mind* came out in the early eighties. But at the time it caused controversy and struggled to gain any kind of academic acceptance. While I was ploughing a career path that still worked counter to my strengths, using my determination as my driving force, Gardner was navigating human brain canals, finding:

'Where individuals differ is in the strength of these intelligences - the so-called profile of intelligences -and in the ways in which such intelligences are invoked and combined to carry out different tasks, solve diverse problems, and progress in various domains.'

Figure 2 – The Eight Intelligences

(Image: (c) marigranula – 123RF.com)

The Eight Intelligences Identified by Gardner

Visual-Spatial - thinking in terms of physical space, as do architects and sailors. Very aware of their environments. They like to draw, do jigsaw puzzles, read maps, and daydream.

Bodily-Kinaesthetic - using the body effectively, like a dancer or a surgeon. A keen sense of body awareness. They like movement, making things. They communicate well through body language and can be taught best through hands-on learning.

Musical - showing sensitivity to rhythm and sound. They love music, but they are also sensitive to sounds in their environments. They may even study better with music in the background.

Interpersonal - understanding, of and interacting with others. These students learn through interaction. They have many friends, empathy for others, and are streetwise. They enjoy group activities, seminars and dialogues.

Intrapersonal - understanding one's own interests, goals. These learners tend to shy away from others. They're in tune with their inner feelings; they have wisdom, intuition and motivation, as well as a strong will, confidence and opinions.

Linguistic - using words effectively. These learners have highly developed auditory skills and often think in words. They like reading, playing word games, making up poetry or stories. They can be taught by encouraging them to say and see words and to read books together.

Logical-Mathematical – reasoning and calculating strengths. They think conceptually, abstractly and are able to see and explore patterns and relationships. They like to experiment, solve puzzles, and to ask cosmic questions.

Naturalistic - These individuals are readily able to recognize flora and fauna, to make other consequential distinctions in the natural world, and to use this ability productively (in hunting, in farming, in biological science). They exercise an important intelligence which has to do with nurturing and relating information to one's natural surroundings.

The Career Apostles

In my own work, based on research, consultation and experience, I have to take the general meaning of the word apostle – an advocate or supporter of a particular policy, idea, or cause. Using the model of Jung's archetypes to determine which grouping the advocate, or client, best belongs to; we together devise the best method, behaviour or approach through recognising the different intelligences defined by Gardner.

I have identified twelve major career archetypes. Remember while one will preside, or two, there are traits in us all that can be developed. Take the knowledge but don't restrict yourself with it, have fun with the ideas. While reading through these descriptions see if you spot your own. You will certainly recognise the archetypes you are not. That's important also.

As some of the most experienced careers advisors know, career guidance is often a process of elimination, and in identifying the roles we are definitely not, we can see more clearly the roles that suit.

As a parent, you might be trying to help your children make important career decisions at this time. We know that parents probably know their children best. These archetypes can be viewed from this perspective also, and perhaps you can gain some insights into what career path might best suit your son or daughter. You might also see the areas that you have in common – the ancestry you gave them, together with the diverging potential of future generations – manifested in your offspring following their individual destiny.

The Carer

Apart from our family predispositions, we also have national characteristics. The Italian love of children, French sophistication, Scandinavian social conscience, British stiff upper lip, German efficiency – while they might be seen as stereotypical, a stereotype has to arise from some measure of truth and impression. So what is it to be Irish?

I remember a friend of mine once telling me that Ireland is a heart nation. A sociologist perspective on Ireland would suggest that this concept dates back to a tradition being passed down from generation to generation. This was based on the need to care for the infirm or older family members in the household. This need was based on a fear of a loved one being placed in the County Home. The seeds were being sown for the younger members of the family to become accustomed to this attribute of care and to invest this attribute/vocation into their future careers (Share and Lalor, 2009).

Another possible reason could be due to the fact that as a country we were subject to eight centuries of oppression. During these trying times, people had to learn to look out for one and other and lend each other a helping hand. Consequently, a high percentage of people in Ireland seem to have a deep sense of caring for others. We are known for our welcome, we are capable of a high degree of expression, and we are interested in people.

Indeed, in a recent comparative survey of career preferences among young people in the UK, the results showed a much lower percentage of respondents interested in the caring professions. Young people in this survey showed a much greater interest in areas such as IT, digital media and the creative careers.

There is no right or wrong of course here. It merely just illustrates the difference in preference. Caring careers cover the health care and social/psychology areas. Health care is very broad and covers areas from nursing to nutrition, from radiography to reflexology. While many strive to gain access to careers in this sector, many don't succeed, as CAO points for courses in Ireland tend to by sky high at times.

But there is more than one way to achieve your archetypal potential.

For many, it is a long, lonely road to the UK to gain the qualifications required to work in these sectors. I am filled with great admiration for these people and their families, who endure geographical distance together with enormous expense, to follow innate traits and desires.

Another area I see major interest in is psychology. One of the key things I have learned is that when people decide to study psychology, they are actually drawn to learning about themselves. I feel this is a significant factor in choosing this discipline. As some will know, only a small percentage of graduates successfully go on to gain places on competitive, psychology post-graduate programmes, but this doesn't seem to deter students. People influenced by this archetype have a very strong drive to understand and help others.

Other popular careers that appeal to the Carer are social work, counselling and, I would add, guidance counselling. All of these careers demand a strong sense of empathy and the ability to listen attentively.

Finally, within these sectors, I find lots of people who seem to have a vocation for helping people with disability. This is often as a result of having a family member with a disability and having had exposure to the problems they encounter in their everyday lives. The interpersonal intelligence is the most relevant here. The Carer is very much aligned with Jung's archetype of the Care Giver.

Carers also have careers in fields of human rights. Our great ambassador of conscience, former President Mary Robinson, is one figurehead of this archetype, someone who has placed their intellect in the service of improving the plight of humanity. Caring put an Albanian woman into an Irish convent and then onto the streets of Calcutta, turning her into Mother Teresa.

Caring is not just a trait that demands sacrifice; it can lead its proponents to be celebrated as the best expressions of humanity.

The Maths Master

I'm sure many of us would like to have been born with the natural ability at mathematics and to have strong numerical skills. As an experienced numerologist, one of the people I studied was the ancient Greek philosopher, Pythagoras, whose triangulation theory has perplexed school students but changed our approach to cartography. He also changed the heavens for all who listened to him. The most important of his theories was the assertion that the earth is not flat, but round. Built on his spherical earth came a new way of looking at the world and new ideas of orbit came to be formed over subsequent centuries.

With his skills in maths and science offering humanity a new way of seeing, Pythagoras could be seen as a figurehead for this archetype, within which people seem to revel in sorting complex mathematical equations.

Also, adept at physics, these high-fliers are set for top end, high earning positions that myself and other mere mortals could never aspire to. They are often the opposite in behaviour to the Carer. For example, these mathematical geniuses in most cases would have little patience for attending to the mathematical needs and concerns of primary school kids.

Destined for careers as actuaries, financial analysts, IT programmers and scientific or mathematics lecturers, people in this category love their gadgets and have all the latest in electronic playthings.

In my experience, a smart appearance is important to them. They choose mathematics, applied maths and physics for their Leaving Cert and in their spare time enjoy documentaries on Stephen Hawking and the Hadron Collider. They get their laughs from watching *The Big Bang Theory*. Later in life, they might align with Jung's archetype, the Sage, who is also known as the Expert and the Scholar.

The Gardner Intelligence in operation here is pretty obviously Logical-Mathematical.

The Number Generator

Closely aligned to a Maths Master, they might not have the visionary genius to come up with a theory of relativity, but they know how to organise the numbers to best advantage. The business, finance and administration sectors are made for the Number Generator. While not as proficient with mathematics, they show a true appreciation of what numbers mean and are extremely well organised around them.

There is nothing more attractive to this type of person than tidying up and reorganising a set of messy accounts, whipping them into shape, and transforming them into a set of clear tables and categories. They love their post-it notes and highlighter pens and can't imagine work without alphabetically indexed and colour

70

coded lever arch files. They populate the banking, insurance and fund accounting corporations of this country.

Working in the public service also appeals to these business administrators. Not only due to the emphasis which is placed on structure, and a clear demarcation between departments, but also very importantly the security and predictability that working in a government department or local authority brings.

Many take the long and often arduous route to becoming a qualified accountant, while others will venture into management positions where they are often quite successful. Here, they can now fully utilise and expand their organisational skills into organising other people.

In this instance, they become aligned with Jung's archetype, the Ruler.

Gardner's Logical-Mathematical ability is once again evident in this category.

Michael Noonan embodies the key traits of this archetype. They might often be background players to a leader, but what they lack in terms of charisma they make up for in capability. Their number crunching and their level efficiency are what organisations and state finances rely on to keep running.

The Planner and Enterpriser

People motivated by this type of work love an event. We could call this category of employment *buzziness*, as there nearly always seems to be a buzz associated with the related work activities they do. They are people-people.

We find them organising conferences and weddings in major hotels, or managing fast-paced retail outlets and leisure centres. They love interacting with people and are ideally suited to roles in customer services and direct sales. In finance, we often find them as qualified financial advisors, giving one-to-one advice regarding mortgages or life assurance.

The image is fundamental to this bracket. They like to wear classic cuts and keep it sharp, a contrast to their strong but considered approach to people. They look the part, and they act it. They are generally positive and enthusiastic about life and work, and one tends to feel uplifted in their company.

As students, however, the planner organisers don't always show a high level of motivation to study. While academically bright, the routine of school and study doesn't hold much appeal for this on the go personality. They are often hard to tie down and sometimes we must be prepared to move with them in order to spend time in their company.

People from this archetypal range often bring their optimistic outlook to enterprise, where they are naturally good at marketing and sales. Many have a leaning towards starting their own business and become self-employed. When they do so, they can often become quite successful. In another variation on this theme, I often meet people attracted to the uniformed roles of Gardai, Defence Forces and Paramedics.

In these situations, accidents and emergencies provide the adrenaline needed to sustain commitment to a role which often involves significant danger to one's own personal safety. The corresponding Jung archetype is the Hero. It's an ego-based drive, centring around the roles of Creator and Innovator, as well as the Magician's role of making things happen.

Our leading hoteliers John and Francis Brennan make this archetype looks effortless.

The Engineer/Designer

Engineers impress me. They seem to have the ideal mix of skills and abilities, and in most cases, they put them to good use. While academically strong, they also have excellent design skills and like to be hands-on with their work. Engineers are behind most of the improvements we see in everyday, modern life. They are leaders in innovation, and they continue to make major advances particularly in the areas of electronic and computer engineering. As our planet warms to a dangerously high level we are now turning to our engineers to find alternative sources of energy and reduce greenhouse gas emissions. Finding a better way is the main motivation for the engineer as they strive to make our world a better and more productive place in which to live.

While design is the core part of an engineer's toolbox, another career in this category that specialises in technical design is that of the architect. Architecture seems to be enjoying a huge surge in popularity in Ireland at the moment with programmes like

Room to Improve, giving us all an insight into the mind of the modern architect. Drawing on Gardner's spatial intelligence, their ability to see three-dimensional shapes and designs both impresses and inspires, while their finished designs can sometimes leave us wondering where exactly did the idea come from.

Not restricted to hands-on roles, engineers often turn their hand to very good effect in management. In fact, the person that has had the single greatest effect on my career is an engineer called Tony Donegan. Tony was without a doubt, the greatest manager of people and resources that I have ever worked with. Not only was he an excellent manager, but he was also a great leader. Strong vision and charisma often accompanies the Leader, and Tony had both in abundance. He was equally adept at communicating with company Vice-Presidents in large corporations and assembly workers on production lines. A proud Cork man, he had an impressive ability to remember names and for making people feel they were highly regarded as individuals.

There is no one archetype or intelligence dominating this career persona. It is probably because of this that engineers are so adaptable. But if I were to choose I would say that Gardner's visual-spatial intelligence is a prerequisite for architecture, while the logical-mathematical intelligence would be central to the diagnostic abilities needed to be a successful engineer.

Robert Mallet is probably Ireland's most famous engineer, and Irishman James Hoban, who travelled far enough in life to design the White House, is another exemplary figurehead.

The Great Outdoors

A percentage of my clients, mainly male, express a strong preference for working in the outdoors. What they do in the outdoors doesn't really seem to matter. The main thing is that they are absolutely sure that they will never be found working in an indoor or office job.

For these people, being stuck behind a desk is literally the equivalent of being in prison, while having an office job has the same appeal working in McDonald's has, to a strict vegetarian.

If you asked Bear Grylls or Ray Mears to hand over their rucksacks you would be taking the key characteristics of this archetype and sublimating it. But they are famous examples of men made for the outdoors.

We find these people in forests and in fisheries and from house construction to horticulture. They are at home on farms or driving machinery and seem to thrive in all kinds of weather. Indeed, for a couple of weeks each year, we seem to envy their bronze, tanned bodies while we trudge towards our artificially lighted and air-conditioned offices.

In terms of Gardner, he originally defined seven roles, but in 1995 he went on the record saying that he would add an eighth intelligence, that of naturalistic intelligence. He describes these people as having the ability to recognise flora and fauna and to use this ability productively in farming, hunting and in the biological sciences.

The dream job for this archetype might be a park ranger on a large country estate where he or she would feel in perfect harmony with nature while being surrounded by native wildlife. David Attenborough, the world renowned naturalist, and BBC's Adam Henson of Country file, speak for this category in noble fashion.

Because school work is almost exclusively desk-bound and indoors, this archetype will have developed an aversion to it, from a very young age. I feel sorry for parents trying to make these students fit in or settle down into the school routine, all to no avail. This outdoor type's main motivation is to finish school and move onto the great world as soon as possible.

The Master Craftsman

These are the doers of the world, gifted with their hands, practical and possessing a strong work ethic. These people are capable of producing high-quality crafts work, often with a very delicate finesse. They take great pride in their work, which is often seen as an extension of themselves. Potential critics will see that they are not welcome where the craftsman has left his mark. If you make the mistake of not appreciating their work they make the mistake of taking it personally.

Qualifying for these careers often takes the route of training for four years in craft-based apprenticeships. Once qualified, the young person will often spend a number of years refining their skills and knowledge, sometimes guided by a master craftsperson. Subsequently many decide to go it alone as sole traders.

Craftspeople love to work with good tools and great materials, especially wood. They will know where to find the best clay, metal and stone for their particular crafts and are prepared to spend long hours bending, shaping and moulding the materials into perfect shape.

From a young age, these students will excel in subjects like woodwork, metalwork, technology and tech graph, showing little or no enthusiasm for non-practical subjects such as languages. Because they tend to be engrossed in their work, many of this archetype, though not all I must emphasise, are not noted for their love of communication with others. Consequently we don't see or hear about these masters in the national media on a regular basis. Rather they like to express themselves by deeds or quality outcomes.

Sadly many of our traditional crafts are dying out as there is no longer a strong demand for crafts such as black-smith or thatcher. However it is nice to see new talents emerge such as Irish Jewellery Designer of the Year, Blaithin Ennis.

Gardner's bodily intelligence is at play in this archetype, allowing these people to handle tools with great skill. We have to consider the rich heritage Ireland has in this area – a walk around the National Museum allows you to have direct contact with the makers of artefacts who took their craft to its highest level in the Golden Age.

Their works speak to us, and for them, still. In the times they lived in, no doubt it was the same. Sometimes I find a higher percentage of Jung's introverts populating this category. They like to let the work speak for itself.

The Teacher

The profession of teaching does not just cover school teachers. Any profession that requires a clear explanation of concepts and ideas can be considered a teaching profession. The teaching archetype attracts confident people with good interpersonal skills. In this instance, I think of adult trainers, conference presenters and sports coaches. The challenge of effective teaching is always one of helping each student get a grasp of the fundamental concepts they need to understand. The best teachers seem to be able to identify the specific needs of each learner and communicate with them on that level. Some students seem to be born with teaching as a vocation. One of the most common things I have heard over the years is something like:

'All she ever wanted to be from a young age was a primary teacher.'

I also find it quite common to have parents who are teachers, to encourage their children to follow suit and it's not uncommon for me to meet families with maybe two or three siblings who have committed to this career. If we are looking for insights into the teaching personality, then we should consider Gardner's multiple intelligences and specifically, the interpersonal intelligence. Students here are defined as those that have many friends, empathy for others and are generally street smart. They are good team players and are sensitive to the moods and feelings of others.

Because teaching is such an important and widespread profession, Gardner is now considering proposing yet another multiple intelligence which is called pedagogical intelligence to cover just the teaching profession.

Good teachers need to be emotionally strong. While we all know about the attractive holidays, many don't witness the stress associated with being a teacher in modern day Ireland. For some who are not equipped with the right blend of emotional intelligence, teaching can be a very difficult and pressurised occupation.

It is not surprising that many gifted teachers have gone on to use their strength and sensitivity to create careers in public life: Roddy Doyle, Brendan Gleeson, Enda Kenny and Eamon De Valera fought in the classroom frontiers, before they forged ahead in fields that took all the skills they had learned in imparting knowledge to minds not always appreciative but always in need of knowledge.

Teaching as a profession can be considered a caring profession and is most closely aligned with Jung's Care Giver.

Chapter 4 – Making the Invisible Visible

The Legal Eagle: Law holds a strong attraction for a specific category of people. Students that express an interest in law also seem to be interested in current affairs. They like to keep up to date with the latest news regarding the economy, and I often find that they are already studying economics or maybe history in school.

They are interested in the media and politics, and some enjoy nothing more than the opportunity to debate their knowledge in competitions with other like-minded students. President Mary McAleese was a professor of law, a human, social and civil rights campaigner and was called to the bar, before becoming a national political figure.

Given her oration skills, it is not surprising that linguistic intelligence is highly developed. Eagles love reading and playing word games and are normally good storytellers. The late Gerry Ryan was a law student before he took the studio by storm.

The seemingly lucrative salaries of the legal profession are a big motivating factor. Students do want to see a fair return for the six to seven years that they will spend studying and training to qualify. Law as a career is often seen as highly prestigious and appeals to those for whom high levels of self-esteem are important.

Law is often a career that a person expresses an interest in from an early stage. It is generally a black or white decision, and those who commit to Law seem to know it is right for them from the start. Sometimes, I wonder why.

Certainly, the recent proliferation of crime programmes on our TV screens has had a definite impact on people's awareness of law as an exciting career option (indeed the same can be said for forensic science). However, the day to day routine of a solicitor in Ireland can be far removed from the drama of the courtroom.

Newly qualified solicitors in Ireland are much more likely to start in a less glamorous role such as that of a conveyance lawyer in a small legal practice. Mary McAleese and Gerry Ryan would have made notes for someone before becoming noteworthy themselves.

The Scientist

Carrying out investigations and a quest to know how this world of ours is put together motivates the Science archetype. Scientists explore the core of our being from neural pathways to

Nanotechnologies. This career covers a broad range of issues, including biomedical, biological, chemical and pharmacological systems. The scientist's precision and accuracy often leads them into inspectorate roles, crucial during wartime, and subsequently refined into modern day quality assurance.

Research is the Mecca for budding scientists. They love the challenge of finding answers and cures to earth's problems, such as malaria and cancer. Microbiologists and biotechnologists, on the other hand, hunt down super resistant bugs such as MRSA in hospitals, and they also try to stay ahead of nature with the development of ever more complex compounds and antibiotics.

Academically strong, the young Scientist will have studied biology and most importantly chemistry. Chemistry explores the building blocks of the universe, and with this knowledge, Scientists have helped to shape the modern world by their introduction of everyday materials such as polymers and polyester. While physics (including the study of astronomy and space science) also forms part of the science family, people from the maths based Archetype are more likely to pursue these as careers.

In some respects, the Science researcher aligns with Jung's Introvert type or with Gardner's intrapersonal intelligence. People with high levels of this intelligence, don't always need other people around them. Because sometimes researchers in science often spend long periods alone, this intrapersonal introversion is often well suited to that role.

Robert Boyle, 'the father of chemistry', was born in Lismore in the seventeenth century, Shackleton, our famous explorer, was exploring for the purposes and progression of science.

The Creative

When asked about careers in the sector, most of my clients answer with the statement: 'I can't draw.' Some take this even further by emphasising the fact that they can't even draw a straight line. Unfortunately, while this is what they experience in their own mind, in truth, we know that every human being is born creative. Sadly because of an education system that is almost exclusively dominated by left brain logical teaching methods, the gift that is their natural birth right has been shut down effectively by the age of ten.

Chapter 4 – Making the Invisible Visible

If only they knew that this negative step could be reversed, then we might live in a much more inspiring and beautiful world. Thankfully however not in all cases and a percentage of people do manage to resist the onslaught on their creative – musical – visual and spatial intelligence, and go on to pursue further studies in these areas.

Flare, exuberance and a passion for the finer things in life, define the Creative archetype. He/she loves to paint, draw and sculpt new designs and they have a strong desire to bring something new into the world of beauty and aesthetics.

Careers in art and design are often a labour of love, and in a lot of cases, artists do not have a regular defined job in the normal sense of the word. This doesn't seem to deter the budding artist or designer in the least, however, as they cannot envision any other way of living their life.

While careers such as graphic design or product design can lead to regular jobs, the path of the person on the artist's way is often one of struggle while trying to stay positive and optimistic about making a breakthrough and leaving a lasting imprint in the world of aesthetics.

Creative careers also encompass creative writing and some aspects of journalism. There are fewer jobs than qualified applicants in pursuit of these, but persistence pays off for this archetype who will succeed if they appreciate the process along with the outcome. Linguistic intelligence is inclined to play a more dominant role within the world of the writer, but it is nonetheless an important part of the family of creative careers.

Apart from our caring DNA, Irish people are known for their writing abilities. There are too many world-famous authors to list, but the tradition continues with modern-day contributors who will one day contribute to the canon of literature. Within the creative careers sector, we also find disciplines such as fashion and visual merchandising. The fruits of their labour can be viewed everywhere from world-class catwalks to local boutiques and market stalls.

You don't always have to have words and degrees to display your talent as a creative. Trades such as hairdressing and beauty therapy have many outlets. For those lucky enough to get involved in the competitive world of film or television or magazine photography – they get the opportunity to show unique looks, from Harry Potter characters to creating looks to make the stars shine in the best light.

I also include cooking as one of the creative careers. Since the explosion of celebrity chefs and food programmes, we have found that the culinary arts are prevalent and employing people all over the world. Master Chef programmes being beamed into our living rooms seem to have added a completely new and exciting dimension to working with food.

The Musician

They used to sit and speculate, upon their son's career,
A doctor or a lawyer or a civil engineer,
My parents and my lecturers could never understand,
Why I gave it up for music and the free, electric band.
(Albert Hammond)

I'm forever amazed at the amount and depth of the musical talent that is evident in Ireland. Almost every student that presents to us lists music as an interest, whether as an instrument player, singer or even just as a listener. Music seems to play a central role in our everyday lives. Many are involved in local music groups and, through competition, have experience in performing from a local Feis right up to the National Concert Hall.

However, for a variety of reasons very few go on to committing to careers as full-time musicians or singers. Lots of musically talented students seem to decide at an early stage that playing music for money is far too competitive or risky for them. They play for home territories or for stress relief.

Some use their singing, acting and dancing skills on stage within the world of theatre and musical theatre. For these, there is nothing like the buzz of opening night for the latest local show. Gods make their own importance, and for committed artists, the effort put in would rival a professional career.

For the musician, the expression is the core. Just because you haven't gone platinum does not mean that you haven't been successful. On the contrary, musicians bring so much to the world. Their performances are often spine-tingling, and they seem to have the ability to raise our spirits to higher levels. Indeed, music is also known for its therapeutic qualities, and a small number of people go on to study music therapy and make it a career option.

Music lovers often like cool careers like sound engineering or creative media technologies. They often form small groups for jamming sessions, with some progressing onto live gigs. Gardner defines this intelligence as musical, rhythmic and harmonic and it is easy to see the attraction of these activities for the music minds. Most seem happy just to be involved in an industry that has been turned on its head with the advent of the Spotify, YouTube and computer generated composition. As for artistic proponents – two letters – U and 2, with a trail of others in their wake.

Figure 3 - Archetypes

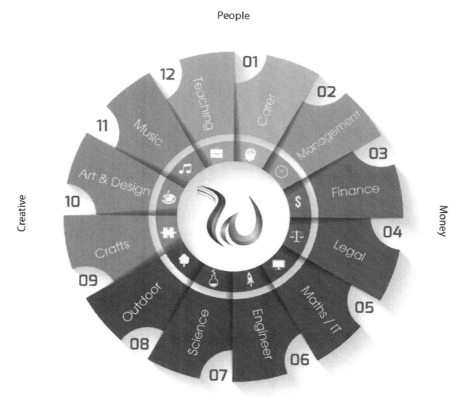

The Twelve Tribes

You might be a blend of these, or you might show singular strength, but these categories speak for one thing. Everyone is a proponent of something and to find it they have to follow instincts.

You may belong to one of the twelve career tribes more than others, but ultimately you are reading this chapter to find out more about you. Take what you like and leave the rest. Don't let a category define you. If you are isolated in your working instincts, seek out those who are more your tribe.

No one is an island. The setting of a career goal will be enhanced by sharing with a likeminded individual, who knows more than most what you are aiming for.

Austerity is No Authority over Love

The mid-noughties downturn in the economy hit homes hard. While politicians read statement after statement of blame and shock in the Dail, while bankers retreated into ivory towers, ordinary men and women all over Ireland lived with the devastation. They rebuilt from the shards of broken homes and lost dreams in the aftermath of a tsunami of poor, often criminal decisions by our political and financial figureheads.

Nobody unless they were employed in public services, escaped the last hit. From 2006 to today, families still deal with the disparity between higher bills and lower incomes. Education today is a cost many find hard to manage. The fees are not gone, just renamed as a 'Student Contribution Fee'; and the related costs to a third level place are higher than they have ever been before austerity arrived.

The downturn changed the way we bank; it changed the way we are governed, it brought a rake of independents into politics and sent a lot of CEO's packing. There were inquiries. There were tribunals. But there were few apologies. There were some prosecutions.

But no one gave the ordinary men and women back the livelihoods and homes they had built trusting in the false – the promises by leaders who should have known far better.

Those public leaders are retired mostly now. The CEOs have part-time consultancy positions and second homes in the sun. The ordinary families affected by the downturn have not had holidays or luxuries. They are about the provision of the basics. But they are also about the provision of the future for their children. Half my client list of young people has at least one parent who had hours cut, salary reduced, business lost, or redundancy announced.

The heroism I am writing about is that people carry on, rebuilding from the ruins of the economy, quietly and to great effect. They get up and do what needs to be done. They do what needs to be done for their children. This is the chief driving force. Politicians and financial leaders, insulated from the consequences of their own actions, talk now about recovery and economic growth. They do not understand that this is not news to the little people. We have made this occur. In trying again after redundancy, in retraining after businesses are lost, in taking any job that comes in, that is how an economy is rebuilt. Not after a decision in Dail Eireann.

We didn't just bail out the banks with our taxes; we worked to buy our country's future back. A chief example of this is the McCarthy family. Two of the hardest hit and hardest working parents I have met. It has been my privilege to know them for five years. Every downturn headline affected them. Lost business. Reduced hours. Unemployment. Retraining. Financial struggle. They haven't just read the headlines. They have lived them.

Both parents in recent years have returned to education. Aine to upskill in Office Technology and Eoin to retrain in the caring professions. There you have two simple statements. But the history that went into that proves the heroism.

They got their PLCs while providing their children with opportunities for degrees.

George Elliot wrote that the greatest heroes lie in unknown graves. Aine and Eoin are examples of the great who will never make headlines. But if they and others like them did, we would have a greater impression of ourselves as people, as individuals working for the greater good.

They are exemplary for their work ethic; they are outstanding parents. They deserve presidential honours. But they are just doing what needs to be done in their view.

'I haven't time to look at how anyone else is rearing their children, or commenting on what they're doing. I am busy taking care of mine.' Aine has a strong spine and a soft voice. 'Eoin and I are committed to them and to doing what needs to be done.'

What needs to be done, in their book, is anything that will help.

'From our first child, the nurse noticed how good a father Eoin is. He would be put his hands under their feet,' Aine states it with her customary simplicity, and it truly affects me. They have a deep love of their four children and for each other. When I praise what I have seen in her family she smiles and says:

'They are great people, all four of them. Each one of them is different, but they have that in common. Whether it means at times we have to push, pull or drag them, we will get them to realise it, and our greatest wish is for them to have good jobs that they enjoy. The first gift of life is health. The second is education. We give them all equal treatment, and we have equal excitement when they pass the milestones and have their own achievements.'

It proves what I see every day. Austerity, which affected us all who were in the private economy, is no authority over parents. Regardless of how much it hurts the purse, regardless of how empty the purse is, they will find a way.

Love is the authority. And it always wins. Aine is the meaning of her name – radiance emanates from this wise, understated and clear-eyed woman. Her manner is as beautiful as manners come. She would never willingly harm anyone. She and her Eoin have lived the values of family and education. Together they live the example of a generation who want to see the next provided with a better life and more opportunities than they had themselves.

'We say to each other we can't expect credit from them right now. We don't need to be credited. It's enough to see them moving ahead.' She shows me a photograph of the four children taken last year at the first of what will be many conferrings for this family. Two young women and two young men. They are close in age and close as a family. They are all at her eldest child's graduation. He is wearing the cap and gown, and the other is smiling as if they are too.

They will succeed. This woman and her husband will make it happen.

Seeing the photograph is moving for me, because Aine and Eoin have sent their three children to me before choosing college courses. The fourth will be in the chair soon. She is doing her Leaving Certificate in 2018. Boy, Girl, Boy, Girl – a perfect family who have lived through imperfect circumstances and made the future occur despite great obstacles.

What comes to me each time I meet with them is that the parents have a strong work ethic, a great intellect and a genius compassion for the rights and lives of their young people. But they have struggled greatly to give them the chances they themselves never received.

A juggling act between grants, loans, consultations, assessments and grinds fees, has delivered the four young people their third level prospects. The numbers don't add up to the family bank account, so a magic has been worked, as it is all over Ireland in households hard pressed by austerity and its consequences.

The word that comes to me about them is alliance. The parents forged one, and they invited their children to join and take part in the decisions around futures that could not even be dreamed about for the parents themselves.

'A friend remarked on how we make decisions by involving the children. We always let them make their own. We guide and advise, but we try to have it in such a way that the ultimate decision is theirs. This generation has all of the opportunities, but they also have all of the pressures. In many ways, though we lacked opportunities when we were our children's age, life was less pressurised.'

Choices were fewer, and there was further between them, but when they presented themselves, choices were simpler. Aine's parents ran a small business which supported three family members. She saw that there was limited finance available for educating her and her younger siblings. Her summer job, after the then Intermediate Certificate at sixteen, saw her intelligence appreciated and the firm simply did not want to lose her at the end of August.

An administrative position that would not normally be offered to someone of her age and stage was hers. This caused a dilemma at home. Her parents didn't want her not to get a Leaving, but they and Aine also saw this was the job she would be offered even after she got one. It would also help the family finances. A priest who was a family friend and had a great respect for the family saw how much Aine was capable of. 'Make sure she keeps up her languages,' was the advice. Aine had a great flair for them. She never studied them again.

Similarly, Eoin, who has a heart of gold and good hands, was going through the Leaving Certificate motions but not interested. He had his eye on an apprenticeship. He did well at this, but when the eighties recession hit, many businesses went to the wall, and his training was finished but so was his position. He ended up taking factory work.

'Looking back sixteen years of age was way too young for me to make a life choice,' Aine looks out of the window and shakes her head. 'There was no guidance at all.'

Eoin was capable of a lot more too, but it just wasn't right or feasible to go on to third level in his family either. Tutorial fees weren't paid then. With accommodation costs and board, it was out of the question to go away to study. So it made the Leaving Certificate feel pointless to him.

'That's why we put all the children in the position of seeing you, Seamus. The choices need to be made by more than the parents.' She points out one of the main points I want this book to make.

And the provision for those choices is up to the parents, which is a huge strain. She and Eoin are the kind of conscientious individuals who put their children way in front of themselves.

Paying for my services is just one of the extras they gave the children all the way along.

'When it's education it always comes back to you,' Aine points out. 'Education should not be based on what you can afford to pay, but what you are capable of. It should help you reach your potential, not take it away. Lots of young people are capable of going further in education, and lots of them don't get the opportunity. That's why we go out on a limb.'

It's a long limb. To put one child through college costs a heavenly fortune. They had three at once.

'Now I know why people have three years between each child! I just wanted them all to grow up together, so there are only eighteen months between all four.'

Over the years since they met, Aine was promoted to a managerial position which fits her wise and observant nature. Eoin took his courage in his hands and set up a construction firm. When the Celtic Tiger was a cub, in the late nineties, they got their chance to make good. But the making good was costing high personally.

'I was working long hours, and I have to say there were times I heard a baby cry when I went out at lunchtime, I would turn around because I just wanted to be with my own children at home. I personally think most mothers would prefer to be.'

It wasn't possible because Eoin was getting his business off the ground and his flexibility and self-employment allowed him to do the pickups and drop-offs that all families revolve around. It's a fairground ride that never stops. Eventually, his reputation spread and the family could afford to make a different choice.

'He said to me he could get more work and I could do less. So an opportunity came up for redundancy in my firm, and we took the chance.'

It worked brilliantly until the downturn brought the whole scheme grinding to a halt, not instantly but eventually. Eoin went from round the clock work to round the clock watching the phone to ring with a job. Aine found work again, Eoin, a natural and instinctive father, went back to working for the family at home. At this point the four were well into primary and then as they began to make the transition into secondary, another financial axe fell. Aine's firm put her on shorter hours.

The strain then really hit because as the eldest was preparing for third level, the only income coming into the house was part-time. Five years later things are far better, but five years ago they couldn't possibly have known that.

Basically Aine and Eoin – self-starters and highly capable – had worked their way up in jobs and in business, but the reality was when the redundancies and downturn came they were competing in an employment market that wanted third level qualification on the CV, not simply experience. This is why their work ethic was then turned to a determination to get training themselves and confirmed their decision to be completely dedicated to their children getting third level qualified.

This belief had its roots in the fourth class of a primary school with one of her children. Aine noticed something: 'They said she wasn't working hard enough. But I knew she was trying.'

An assiduous process, fought by Aine and Eoin, and an assessment confirmed that she was dyslexic. Despite being on one income, they paid for private tuition which helped greatly, but it was the first sign that making an ideal real, can mean real sacrifice.

No holidays. No luxuries. Tight budgeting. It's okay to write it, but to live it for twenty or more years is challenging. There is no catastrophic tragedy to cope with, but the facts of the resolution can wear a parent down.

'I am a detail person. That's needed. I took care of the details and Eoin, and I both took care of the needs for various grinds, support and so on. Eoin is great at finding out the information, and I can do the form filling and processing.'

Education of four children holds the paperwork load of a small country. Taking care of the day's needs has led to this fine young man going to do a course suited to his taste. By 2018 three of the McCarthy's will be fully qualified. The fourth will be in the first year of a suitable programme.

'Coming to you confirmed what two of them really wanted to do and showed the other two what they have to do. Sometimes a young person will let it all happen. Other times a young person will make it happen,' she has a great way of summing things up.

They are all individuals in the McCarthy household, playing to their strengths and following their interests. Next year, for the first time, the load lightens, and the parents are planning their first holiday. But it's a milestone that the youngest will be in a college dorm by then.

'It hits me with a bang sometimes,' Aine admits. They have been hard times but great times. She and Eoin sometimes walk the beach, and a constant topic is the four, how they have achieved and what they can build on.

I have a sense, while their children are thankful today and say it to their parents, in years to come the four young McCarthy's, the four evangelists of two people's dedication that went beyond limits, creating a closeness and support that these young adults will benefit from for the rest of their days, will raise their parents on their shoulders and carry them as heroes.

5

FROM LEADER
TO LISTENER

Chapter 5

From Leader to Listener

The Role of Parents

 Parental guidance for a teenager is a phase where your support still means everything, but your input is not as valid as it was when they thought you ruled the world. Parents of children who are in their mid to late teens notice that while their need for parents is great, it is different from offering you their every need. The goal posts don't just change; they're uprooted and put in different parts of the pitch. It is still the same game, but the rules have been reinvented.

They are making their own way more in the world. Now you help them negotiate it.

Parents want the very best for their children. After all, they have invested a vast amount of attention and energy into bringing their child to this important transition stage. They deserve the best possible outcomes available, even if only for the massive financial investment they are now about to make in a lot of cases, without any significant grant aid from the powers that be. But, sometimes parents need to step back from their own expectations and make sure that the needs of their soon to be young adults are being met in relation to a future lifetime of work and labour.

Twenty years ago, when I started my work advising students on various careers, I assumed that students would be my customers. I learned very quickly that in the case of student career guidance, their parents are. Parents are the major stakeholders in the career guidance process. Career guidance would be a very straight-forward process if it was only a matter of matching student's interests with their aptitudes. However, there is a third factor at play here and a very important one. That factor is employability. How likely is it that the student is going to have a job at the end of their college degree, training course, internship or apprenticeship?

Career advisors must always be conscious of employability, and this certainly makes career guidance for the young person a little more complicated. A short case study might illustrate this fact more clearly.

Jack came to me for assessment some time ago. He was very interested in field sports and excelled in soccer and rugby. Jack's main interest was in pursuing a course in Sports Science. Following our discussions, he realised that there were very little actual job opportunities resulting from this degree, but because he loved sports, he was determined to do it. Enter Jack's mother. When Jack's mother heard he was about to select a degree in Sports Science, she became visibly upset. She herself had a very strong work ethic, and she couldn't conceal her disappointment because she felt he wouldn't be employable. Furthermore, she reminded me of this fact and told me this was why she brought Jack to me.

She thought he might listen to me. But Jack had friends going to the University of Limerick, and he had no intention of going anywhere else.

There was a stand-off between parent and child, as I so often see this in my practice. At the end of the day, we as career advisors don't make decisions for people. Arbitration between two conflicting parties is only achieved by both sides giving ground. The guidance counsellor can provide the best quality information around interests, aptitudes and employability. At that stage parents and students must make the decision themselves.

So I try, in most instances successfully, to get the conflict resolved on the court steps. What works best is if both parties walk a mile in the other's shoes. Parents are endless but not limitless in their support. Their children are often expected to show the responsibility of an adult while taking the instruction of a child whose age is still in single digits.

Jack had an ability - sport, coupled with an instinct - sports science. What his mother could not control was the outcome. He and his mother were keen to tug me to either side of their chasm. Both felt their intuition was one hundred percent right. There is a way to resolve this. Listening! Did I mention listening?

Did I also refer to being heard?

By and large, in our practice, we see three main approaches from parents towards their children selecting college courses and careers. I want to examine these approaches in a little more detail.

'We just want her to be happy, and we'll back her in whatever decision she makes.'

This approach seems to be honest and comes from parents who see happiness and peace of mind as most important for their child. They often say things like:

'We don't want to see her under any unwanted stress. There's enough of that in the world today.'

'Well, we want him/her to be happy, but we do want to see them get a job and be able to support themselves when they leave college.'

The second approach sounds like the first, but the added proviso at the end is the chief indicator. It is often clarifying a more subtle expectation. While the parents remain open to possibilities, some of this appears to be window dressing. Parents are agreeable to a point as long as it fits certain criteria such as college qualification and jobs. Indeed in a minority of cases, parents seem to be hell-bent on a particular college and nothing less will suffice.

'We have told him/her that we expect them to get a meaningful qualification that leads to direct employment where he/she will be able to get a job and support him/herself.'

In this situation, at least we are all clear on the desired outcome, a solid honours degree, leading to a career with a proven track record for promotion and of course an increasing salary to match. No Mickey Mouse degrees here for these parents. They are often well versed in career guidance and are taking this opportunity to ensure that all of their well-founded research and knowledge will be put to good use. In addition, they will be playing a central role in organising the important work experience for their child, more about that later.

Nursing Angela's Expectations

Sometimes, the advice given by parents can be even more specific. Consider the case of Angela who comes to me for assessment. Scenario A: Angela's mother is a qualified nurse. During the assessment she states openly:

'I'm a nurse myself, and there's no way I'd let her go into it. Not the way things are at the moment, so much pressure with very little thanks and not to mention the HSE.'

Scenario B: Angela's mother is a qualified nurse who sees her daughter in the uniform working on a ward also:

'I'm a qualified nurse myself, and I've always loved it as a profession. Angela is a very caring girl, and I think she would make a great nurse, but it's her decision.'

Two very different pieces of advice you'll agree. I see and hear this all the time, and it's not just nursing. I hear it from Gardaí, teachers, accountants. Sometimes it even depends on the day and how things might be going at work in that particular week!

You will notice the only person who doesn't speak in these scenarios is the one making career and college choices.

Angela's mother after a night shift in A&E with a lot of Saturday night drink-related incidents might be saying stay away. Angela's mother, who had saved the life of a young mother on the shift, might be saying it's the best job in the world. But only Angela really knows if she wants to be a nurse.

The thing that qualifies Angela's mother to give an opinion is her education. She puts this alongside her love and predicts a future that really needs to be in Angela's hands. At the very least it should be stated that Angela and her mother are united in one thing – Angela's future is hugely important. The opportunities that come for her will be backed by love and interest all the way. These are priceless.

Work Experience

Without a doubt, those students that have the opportunity to participate in meaningful work experience, have the best chance of making successful career choices. But, to get these opportunities, parents have to become active in organising placements. This means calling in some favours and using all your contacts. Left to their own devices, students seem to get swallowed up by large companies and are often ignored. So many times, when quizzed about their experience, they inevitably give me the answer that they:

'Didn't really learn anything. I mainly just made the tea, tidied up some old files and did some photocopying.'

For those students lucky enough to have personal contacts, they often get paired with a mentor who takes the time to give them an idea of what it is actually like to work as for example, an accountant or Engineer. Hospital contacts are also invaluable for placements and entry onto quality programs such as the Mini Med. These are worth their weight in gold to the prospective aspirant in careers in the healthcare sector.

So, as a parent, if you want to make a meaningful contribution to the process of guiding your child, find out the broad areas they seem most interested in. Then get busy calling your friends in IT, architecture or education, and see about organising some quality work experience for your child. It can make a big difference.

The Unqualified Qualified Parent

Sometimes, the parents that accompany the child do not feel they can offer anything at all. This is another area we must address. For a huge variety of reasons, there is a whole generation of Irish parents who did not have the access or opportunity offered to the twenty-first-century child. So they treat a career guidance meeting as an interview – they are frightened, intimidated and often want to get out as quickly as possible.

Their only objective is to leave, having helped their child, but without being embarrassed by what they feel they lack. They chiefly lack confidence as their children have already exceeded their education level. The parent feels powerless like they have little to contribute to the ongoing success and progression of their beloved child.

There is also a misperception on the part of the child, who has listened to the parents claiming they can't support, that they must go it alone. The child, therefore, makes choices beyond their years, which a qualified career guidance professional could assist them with.

But the fact that the session is paid for, is attended and is fed into at all, is down to the love that keeps our planet going – parental. Every so-called unqualified parent who bothers to make the time, pay the fee and put the option of doing so in front of their children, has already given them the sun, moon and stars through their belief.

So the career guidance service needs to empower and include the parent of the career starter. It's like sending your child on an ocean liner in the days of emigration where you thought you could do little else and might never be of use again. The piece of paper is only one part of an education. The life experience of the parent, who didn't have the chance their child now has, is an important contribution both to the prospects of the seeker and their self-worth in the present moment.

It's, therefore, the role of any guidance professional worth their training, to listen to the parents and to get the parents and child listening to each other. It's all teamwork and will save years of tangents.

No one knows a child like a parent, even the educationally unqualified parent knows a child's strengths, and weaknesses, fears and ambitions and is therefore eminently qualified in ways that will never be given certification but are more important than any piece of paper. If you get up out of bed to an alarm clock, to put food on the table for a family, work as many hours as you can, come home shattered and take a child to an activity, or help them with something to a point in education where you feel yours stopped, then you are as qualified as someone with a doctorate to support your child's continuing life. If you are going without holidays or days out, to get school books; if you are doing with less because you want your child to have more, you have a parenting PhD.

Communicating with your Child

Don't mistake a teenager for an adult person. Children often shut down at the age of between 15 and 16, and I often have to act as an honest broker. They're upset, confused and won't talk to

95

parents. These same parents are distraught trying to get them to open up.

But in this most turbulent decade of all, communication is the key to all concerns. You just have to keep talking. Even if in their youthful moments your children tell you that you haven't a clue, they know that you are clued into their needs. They might not be able to express it at this turbulent time where they are searching for their own identity.

Use every opportunity available to get some one to one guidance, maybe while driving to training or one of the places where parents end up in a car with their child. It's a classic captive audience scenario, and eventually, they get bored and start to talk.

Put on your helmet, take the shower of insults and get to work. Listen to your child's fears and future concerns. Find every spare minute to govern their grievances with action.

I often witness conflict when parents and children are together in my office. I offer my support. While there is conflict at times, at other times there is a joy. Why? It's finally here. The thing you changed the nappies for, got up in the middle of the night to do, the thing you brought a child up for. Your child is almost an adult, is a young adult. Has a boy or girlfriend. Has an adult future ahead. This is a miracle.

You can't force an adult awareness into a young adult's mind. But be careful as you can give it your fears by highlighting the pitfalls over the possibilities. As you can see, as parents to these aspiring adults, you can have a profound influence on their decisions. You cannot underestimate the influence that you as parents exert.

You need to be aware of how much influence you actually have and use this knowledge wisely. Your role, of course, is very valuable, but only in helping or assisting the child in this very important and often difficult decision.

Allow the realities to be seen. You are parents. They are children. They listen less visibly. They sometimes listen impatiently. They ignore. They still hear every word you say.

'Sure, they don't really know what they want.'

This is a mantra that I hear time and time again. When I started my work as an advisor, this statement used to bug me a lot really. Of course, at that time I was hell-bent on sorting out every seventeen-year-old that came my way, with permanent solutions that would last a lifetime. Now I'm not so sure, and I feel that there is some truth in this old mantra.

For me, teenagers have a very limited perspective on life. They are often swayed (and often very wrongly) by their peers, while others choose their models from a variety of online and streamed sources. None of this has much to do with the real world. This is because they are seeking role models beyond you. They are going for advice beyond yours. It is often two-dimensional in the case of the online influence. It is often misplaced in the case of peers. But it is them trying out the world for themselves. Making the mistakes you made. They are listening to a small frame of soundbites, but that is because they are not yet fully in the world.

Advise, don't preach. Believe in the best of what you see in them.

The Graduate Student

Much as I love working with young minds and hearts and futures, I also love working with adults. Through their work and general life experience, they have a much more realistic and rounded view of the world and as such are in a much stronger position to make better decisions. For sure, the experience of being away at college for three to four years is very valuable and in some cases, more valuable than the education itself. So many employers are now saying that universities and colleges can't seem to give graduates the essential skill of common sense, but that's another discussion.

Consequently, in many cases, I feel that, unless you were born with or came to your sense of destiny young, it's when the students graduate from their degree that they are in a position to make realistic career choices. As such, one of the most important pieces of advice we can give to Leaving Cert students in Ireland now is whatever you do, get a good solid honours degree. At least then, you will have a meaningful qualification from which you can launch your career.

Masters Degrees made Popular

In the late eighties, the company that I worked with at the time recruited a scientist who had a master's qualification. This person was almost held in reverence, so rare was it then to be qualified to that level. We were all reminded by management that he was very special and we were lucky to have him on the staff. You could almost hear people speaking about him in hushed tones on the corridors. Nowadays it's almost expected that you have one.

Masters degrees became very popular during the recent recession. With little prospect of work, many graduates took the postgraduate route rather than joining the lengthening dole queues. That trend seems to have become the norm. Young students almost seem to take the masters for granted, and some of them state openly to me they would rather do a general degree first, before deciding then which masters they want to do. This has become more and more popular now than committing to a specific primary degree.

A master's degree can be costly, with fees ranging anywhere from €5,000 to €25,000 for some of the more prestigious courses and colleges. With pretty much no grant aid available, many students opt to borrow. This, of course, brings me to another area, where parents are heavily involved in their son's and daughter's careers, and that is the area of providing funds and finance.

Soaring Education Costs and the Child of Prague

Parents are investing heavily in their children's education. Some could face a huge burden, with two or three students away at college simultaneously if they were born close together. Other parents find a way around the punitive points system to give their child a chosen career. These days the Child of Prague, a statue we prayed to, to stave off rain and other misfortunes, is fully human and trying to become a doctor or vet.

Parents put their students through medical school or veterinary training in Prague or Budapest, and many don't have much change to show from an investment close to €90,000 at the end of this decision. But, because they want the best for their children they somehow get by, and I have the greatest of admiration for the sacrifices they make. Add to this costs of private grinds, educational psychology assessments and maybe a year or two at a private school, and it's no wonder education takes a massive percentage of parents' disposable income. But, as these parents know, the money means nothing to see the child happy and progressing into their true interests.

A very strong example of this is Mary and Richard, who came in with one of their two children – Stephen – for consultation on his future path. They had sunk their entire capital, not just into his third level route, but had taken the view that education came first even when he was a junior infant.

He presented as a bright, sensitive young man in the making, who matured early emotionally but found the school system too regulated for his highly imaginative approach.

'Work with the soul also, please. Not just the goal,' his mother asked, and father corroborated. The couple are highly qualified and have worked in third level institutions as lecturers, among other professional roles. They are also high achievers academically who saw that qualifications don't always qualify you to believe in yourself.

'I left school having gone through it as part of the A stream all the way, won awards and medals and represented the school at sport and debating events. And I left without any confidence.' Mary states.

'I won a scholarship to go to a prestigious private school. It was awful.' Richard adds.

They picked their way through work and education choices, with a sense that something of themselves was missing, but because they were both talented and approachable, they were promoted quickly and found themselves in high status, well-paid positions that they were not entirely suited to.

'There was a high level of administration in my previous role,' Richard explains. 'I'm more academic than administrative. I love learning, but I also know that my experience at school taught me that I was a little stupid. This was confirmed as my parents were hugely disappointed in my plummeting grades from the school that was the Holy Grail for recruiting future key players in society.'

What Richard was, it appears, was ADD – they call the condition in their family Attention Dynamic and Different. Both are familiar with and employ the multiple intelligences theory, to their raising of their sons and their own teaching methods. So, what are committed educators, who clearly have their son's best interest at heart, using a guidance counselling service for? They know that mentoring of a teenager is something that cannot be done with only two voices.

'The more Stephen hears from other committed adults, the more he grows in his own knowledge and learns to take on different perspectives.' Richard insists.

Stephen, I quickly established, had an awareness beyond his years. This will prove useful when he is in his twenties, but for now, he has struggled to find a group of friends who suit.

'I can make friends, but I often find them childish,' he admits.

There is also the fact that he is a gentle young man, with a high degree of sensitivity.

'I just am not cut out for school. The bullying is normal. Teachers, even when they really are good teachers, can't control what happens at lunchbreaks.'

His parents took him out of school for a year, to get some perspective.

'He was only going to experience himself negatively if he continued as he was in that framework,' Richard points out. 'The things he was most interested didn't feature as a part of the curriculum. He just lost heart.'

'We moved house to find the right schools, effectively putting all our life savings into schooling, plus all our disposable income. We shop in second-hand shops and buy second-hand everything to give a first-rate education. Sadly, none of it worked. He would have kept going, but he was more and more withdrawn. So we gave him a year to figure things out, with some exams being taken, but mostly to get some time to reflect and develop life skills.' Mary explains.

It was hard for the parents because they were watching a highly intelligent young man struggling to meet his full potential. 'That's where you came in Seamus! We saw you were thinking at the same deep level, not just about choices but about why people make them.'

Recently, the couple sat down to work out a new critical path for their children. In doing so, they totted up the figures spent in finding the right primary and secondary schools and moving to be near them.

'We suffered disastrous negative equity losses at the time and had to cash in all the little policies. In order to keep going we had to work extra jobs,' Richard recounts. 'I had two jobs, one full-time and a part-time lecturing position at weekends.'

'There was one point in 2010 where I was working ten different contracts,' Mary shakes her head.

What is priceless for them is Stephen is facing up to a future with a new degree of optimism and a grounded sense of what that might be.

'I will never look at the world in the same way again,' he said to his parents after one guidance session when we set goals for a month and also for life.

He is sixteen and heading back into the education system to get the broad-based qualifications which will add to his future. He wants the paperwork to support his intentions and shows purpose in his choice of college for the autumn.

'I will do this because I have to and because I know that doing final exams for school in a college environment suits me. I'm not put off by hard work.'

In this year out, which he calls a year in, he has done two college courses in music technology, some academic exams and a qualification in music. During this year he also learned to compose, play an instrument, paint, decorate, do mind maps, journal, started running seriously and did some work experience:

'I want to find work that makes me feel like I'm of use. I want to keep my music central, and I'm not afraid of failing. I keep trying, and I will get there because I don't expect to get to produce records, or record music in a hurry. I will do related work in the industry because I'm not afraid of hard work. I like it. It never feels like work to me.'

The career guidance sessions showed Stephen he is an adult in the making and his faith in himself is the vital ingredient. His parents have full admiration for him.

'He will succeed at whatever he tries because he will try for long enough,' Richard voices and Mary agrees wholeheartedly.

Both parents worked to organise opportunities which have opened up his mind to what being in the world means.

6

MOTIVATION – LIVING YOUR PRESENT

Chapter 6

Motivation

Living your Present, Tracking your Future

'What lies behind us and what lies before us are tiny matters..... compared to what lies within us.'
Ralph Waldo Emerson

 You are so much more than you can ever imagine. Your potential for greatness came with your first breath. But life is a conversation between survival and dream fulfilment. As a career guide, I have realised the happiest clients are those who turn their dreams into plans. They take action on their deepest desires, having identified them through the analysis of their predispositions – see Chapter 4 on archetypes – and their individual inclinations. Often they come in expecting one thing and leave with another.

Do you do aptitude tests? Converts to: *What is my true aptitude? What working role most reflects who I am?*

This is a high question, and it is rooted in being, not doing. Before anything, you are a person. But you may have developed an untruthful or inapt persona to carry you through your days. You might be a pilot sitting at a desk, or an entrepreneur in the civil service.

Some people come in wanting to make a difference, which is different to being successful if your work is something you're not ultimately suited to. Consider the case of Marie.

"I want to make a difference."

Marie has had a very impressive career to date. She graduated from UCD with a Degree in Economics and joined City Bank in London straight from college. She had a very competitive salary, before returning home to Ireland after five years to join the Bank of Ireland's Lending Division. Opportunities to rise in the ranks were plentiful, and Bank of Ireland paid the hefty fees for her to complete an MBA at the Smurfit Business School.

Marie is now thirty-five. She is on a six-figure salary but feels very empty. She is proud of what she has achieved so far. Her days are full on and often very challenging. But of late she has been wondering, apart from the attractive salary and the seemingly great lifestyle, is there anything more to life and career than this?

A people person, she enjoys meeting new clients. Recently, she volunteered for a month-long stint with street children in Mumbai, very challenging and completely alien to her desk-bound working life at home, but she got so much from it, it was life-altering. Observing people fight for the most primary of human needs, makes her realise a lot of her time furrowing in the world of finance has been an absorption rather than an aspiration. She feels now that this is what she really wants to do in the world, to make a contribution to humanity and start to make a difference to people.

Marie is currently completing an all point's survey on her life. Now is the time to commit to something in the caring areas. She thinks that if this doesn't happen within the next year or two, it probably won't happen at all. So she comes for consultation because two heads are better than one, even one as clever and capable as hers. There is a sense of the self-actualisation coming, and so she needs clear direction on what areas would best suit her caring and empathic inner self.

Her month in India pre-empted this feeling. She got to the bridge before she felt it would collapse. Sometimes, people spend their whole lives climbing the corporate ladder to reach the top, only to realise when they get there, that their ladder was against the wrong wall. Why do people stray so far from themselves?

It's a question of motivation. We are part of a society that less than two hundred years ago starved. We are part of people who had all choices and chances taken away from. Our great-grandparents considered themselves lucky if they could put food on the table. Young adults today have already lived through two big recessions. Anyone over forty has worked through them both. We have watched property prices soar and plummet, the growth economy is often like a paper plane that flies, but you can never tell where and when it is going to land.

If your father and mother grew up without secure employment, were underpaid, the higher motivations are not what they will preach. They will talk to you about getting a good job. So your motivations will be informed by the underlying need to have a roof and a bed and a full belly. The impetus to be something risky may induce a fear reaction in adult guides of young people.

Similarly, if your parents were risk takers, they will not be as afraid of risk in situations and see it as part of life. If they are strong on you being yourself, they will push you to be all you can be. If they know how hard it is to remain individual in a world that demands a certain amount of career conscription, they will sometimes turn sour when you express the desire to be something truly different.

The motivations of a society and a person are governed by the need to continue.

So we can sometimes find ourselves living within parameters we ourselves did not create, but which are imposed on us through social and economic conditioning and conditions. However, there are people who would prioritise a job they love over the take-home pay. For some, the priorities are the other way around.

We, as individuals, need a framework to understand the ancestral and authoritarian input into our motivations.

Abraham Maslow

Abraham Maslow forged his hierarchy of human needs in the depths of the Second World War when survival wasn't guaranteed. He developed it, not watching the whole world, but the healthiest and most innovative fraction of it. By the mid-1950s he was ready to give us the framework we still use today to understand the societal motivation and the person operating within it. He died in

1970 when the world had gone through the biggest geopolitical changes ever encountered in a century. There was more to come, and like Gardner, who updates his intelligences as our economic, education and social environments develop, Maslow might have had more to say in relation to the values. You could almost split each category into subcategories in the technology era, but the basic motivational truth is the same for the human race from the Neolithic to now.

Figure 4 - The Maslow Hierarchy of Needs Pyramid.

Geography has a lot to do with this also. A worker in North Korea is not going to consider the entire pyramid in the same way an employee in the IFSC. But believe it or not, both still have to consider traps of circumstance. The Financial Services Centre employee may be a farmer at heart. The North Korean might be a closet capitalist dying to play the stock market and dying if they take the risk of eschewing the communist society. One has a chance at change, the other little.

But they both have to actively consider how to unlock their true potential within their constraints and constructs. So they have to look at their motivations and what arrows they are pointing to in terms of exhibiting, enacting and exploiting their full individual potential.

What Motivates our Behaviour?

From necessity to strong spiritual values – Maslow considered the entirety. Broad motivation theory is just that – broad – it is rarely ever as simple as a graph. But, as with the archetypes which give us a societal understanding in terms of which group we belong to, looking at the framework of motivation in this chapter, promotes and enhances our individual understanding and gives us our career and life guide ropes.

Maslow's Hierarchy of Needs tried to offer the world at the time not only a broad spectrum of analysis of human behaviour but also an image that connected the most basic needs with the most complex. So he came up with the pyramid. The implication was the higher we climb, the more evolved our emotions and desires. But the needs are all part of the one structure and therefore the whole structure. We can exhibit basic and complex needs at once. Einstein, one of the chief examples of self-actualization Maslow based his model on, had a torrential private life from time to time and deeply spiritual as well as scientific values. Nobody is perfect, and in fact, contemporary and current critics of the pyramid would argue it is based on ideals that most cannot achieve.

What Maslow offered was to further previous explanations of behaviour, and to look specifically at what motivates humans. His thinking was following on and encompassing Freudian theories of primitive desire, Jungian theories of collectivism and Einstein's theories of relativity. He took a measure from all these complexities, and he created a simplicity which has stood time's test because it holds powerful symbolic value.

His diagram is used in education from secondary school level right up to PhD because it gives us if not an entirely real truth, a very real and instant understanding of the complexity of behaviour.

At the time his books were revolutionary in a new world order where borders were being redrawn and new global organisations beginning. He proposed a new and global approach that explains our actions, motivated firstly by the need to fulfil a series of desires or needs as seen in this pyramid diagram:

The pyramid represents the way in which we strive for basic desires starting at the base of the formation, and once each of these is fulfilled, we work our way up to the ideal tier of *self-actualization.*

Applying Maslow's Theory

The amount that is written on the theory and the theories of the theory run to millions of impressions at this point, but here are some simple keywords in relation to each need and its expression in the individual.

Survival – Safety and Energy

The first step is always the hardest, and for a large proportion of our global population, this basic human need is still a luxury they will not always be given.

We need air, water and food to survive in the world.

This still lives on in the animal kingdom, and to witness this at first hand, just watch the great migration across the plains of Africa from season to season. We migrated in this way once. The early humans, the hunter-gatherer's, roamed further and further from their origins in their search to find food. Our work then was all about eating, reproducing and finding a safe spot to sleep. Safety, staying healthy and having the energy for flight or fight are the underlying motivations of this human need.

Shelter – Security and Ownership

We began with a less populated planet. As the population grew, the roaming of the hunter-gatherer was not always possible and the terrain needed to offer us more sustenance in order to keep ourselves and our progeny warm, safe, dry and fed.

The farmer gene in us ignited out of this chief motivation and developed, and we decided to settle in one spot. We started to build shelters to keep us warm, and we learned to use tools. Our enclosures were no longer natural but built. We were becoming maintainers.

Nowadays, we pay others to build our homes, and we call this payment a mortgage. In some cases, this investment is going to take us twenty-five to thirty years to pay off, or one-third of our lifetime, so now we work largely to pay for our shelter.

The desire to own, to have security in this ownership, had been born. It is with us still whether it is a wattle and daub hut and accompanying livestock or a detached home with a new car.

Acceptance – Involvement and Belonging

As we ceased moving, we had more time to engage. We were more involved with each other as individuals. This evolved into the most basic of emotional needs - to belong.

As industries, armies, faiths, cities, empires, countries, trade, culture and arts were founded, the institutions behind all these expressions needed people to work for their agendas. People answered fully in order to survive, and the sense of belonging was paramount over individual desires. They were involved with the greater good, and individual good was a concept on the other side of a sea for the most part.

Today it is the same principle. With our basic needs fulfilled, we then look for acceptance. Initially, we seek acceptance from our family and friends. If we feel loved and accepted, according to Maslow we can move on to the next level. If not, we can struggle to find meaningful relationships.

This need applies to any congregation – from work to womb we basically want to be part of something, and it is when we evolve that we begin to countenance risking our opinion in group environments.

The reason we would do this is that we have seen that if we are to be self-fulfilled entirely we will often have to be unpopular temporarily. If we can put our efforts into this uncomfortable stage, we step up the pyramid.

Self-esteem – Value and Respect

Everybody likes to be liked, but everyone has a need to be also valued, and this is reflected in Maslow's fourth level. He identified the need to be liked as *lower esteem*, fitting in with the previous pyramid step. This involves the need to be loved and valued by our friends, family and co-workers. This is where you are still, as with the last step, but there is more need to be respected.

Higher esteem is more difficult to fulfil, with a need for confidence and faith in ourselves. This is where you achieve self-respect through the assertion of personal values. Even if those values are not valued by groupings or individuals, your ability to hold true to it wins admiration. This, in turn, gives you greater esteem, while making you less prone to waver from outer influences. The world is set up in a way that most people get their self-esteem from others.

Just look at the stars on our sports fields or our TV screens, we adore them and shower them with attributes like All-Star or film icon. They are no longer just their name, or what they do, but the reputation attached. Of course, we also try to emulate them ourselves, in the hope that we too will be esteemed in our community.

This and the previous steps in the pyramid mark the transition point between physiological and experiential needs. Our physical hunger pangs are replaced by more complex needs, one of which is a satisfying career and today we will move to obtain it instead of sticking with the job for life. Certain careers also feed the hunger for improved self-esteem. The higher the profile, the more people will want the job. It is not the job itself but the image of the job we aspire to.

Years ago, we doffed our caps to the priest or doctor. Now we greatly admire the company CEO or perhaps the Dragon's Den entrepreneur. We envy the trappings of those who have made it and wondered, as the saying goes:

'Has God lost my file?'

So much of human endeavour, blood, sweat and tears go into climbing the career ladder for this reason.

Self-Actualisation – Seeing More than Self

Self-actualisation? What does it actually mean, this term that is bandied about so liberally in a postmodern age? As stated at the beginning of this chapter sometimes people spend their whole lives climbing the corporate ladder to reach the top, only to realise that their ladder was against the wrong wall. This is what this level is all about, even when we appear to have it made, Maslow reminds us that we are not quite complete as yet, the final development awaits us.

Ultimately, our main purpose on Earth is to find out what we are doing here and the reality of who we are as a species. Most never reach this step, as along the way they have lost their inner compass for chiefly fiscal reasons. They might be putting the next generation's needs first; they might put a roof over their own head and be unable to consider anything else. Whatever the reason the pressing need is to survive in a market-driven economy where the market keeps changing. This puts untold pressure on our biological needs and leaves aspirations to another time and life.

The struggle to survive even at a time when we are advised it is a given, often can leave certain individuals very little time to look inward and question why are they living the life they currently are. But for some, these questions have been to the forefront from an early age, and they hunger to find their truth. Some follow this path from an early stage. They see the rat race as a senseless pursuit of material things, none of which will give them lasting happiness. Many are judged negatively by society and are often referred to as drop-outs and hippies.

That is by the narrow band viewing them of course. More than one of our poets, playwrights and authors were school refusers. Many an Oscar winner was told they were a write off in education. For most others, they try to work their way through work, family and mortgage commitments.

As the decades move, as we pass through peak experiences where we glimpse the happiness we might have, we find there is more to life than merely changing the car. Oftentimes the clarion call will present as a crisis, but the invitation is always to become more.

Self-inquiry, self-actualization, the possibility of working towards a more ethical or authentic self is possibly the ultimate life purpose. It doesn't mean we turn our back on work, to find a pair of sandals and a pilgrimage. It means we choose to find a way of working that expresses us as we are, and to give the world the advantage of our stimulus, not to dull and deaden it. In my own life, I believe all the step changes that occurred to me along my journey were choreographed to bring me to the point of serious self-enquiry.

While self-actualisation may sound a bit far out into the future for most of us, let's get back to talking about the career changes that will take you to the last step of need – the need to achieve your full potential.

Every step takes us nearer to that goal. What may be useful here is to take a look at some of the main reasons as to why adults come to me seeking a career change. Nearly all of these scenarios are preceded by words such as:
'I never really knew what to do with my life, and I didn't get any career guidance at school.' Then after this most common of phrases, the following lines form the slogan every career counsellor expects to hear at some stage in their practice.

'I fell into this job.'

Joe arrives at the office. I can sense he is nervous. Am I going to ask him about his Leaving Cert, will there be IQ tests? It takes me a while to settle him down, and we chat about the game on Sunday. When he is more relaxed, I ask him to tell me his story.

'Well, I left school and was very unsure about what to do. I thought about a PLC course, but then there was a job going at my Uncle's company. I thought I would take that for a year or max two, before college, when I was clearer about what I wanted to do.' Joe gets restless as he remembers.

'But, then the company got busy. There was a lot of overtime, and I was making good money. I got a nice car, and I kept putting off college.'

Of course, one year slips into the next:

'Before I knew it, I'm married and building a house,' Joe looks out the window. It's hard to face the feelings and the events that are not bad in themselves but didn't always add up to him as he might have been if he had followed his instinct. Still, he has his physiological needs answered, and some experiential; he is being loved and accepted by wife, by work, by the community. It's a good life. Many would wish for it. But the crisis is about to call.

'The job is fine, and I'm well looked after, but I've known nothing else. The last year was quiet, and some lads were let go. I'm wondering could it be me next and I'm scared. I feel like now is finally the time for me to get some qualifications and see if I can do something that I'd really like in my life.'

Joe is about to make a big difference in his own life. He pre-empts redundancy and gets himself into college before events overtake. For the first time, he is self-determining his own big picture. It feels risky. But he is very much alive.

He was good at running the risk, but he might have a chat with my next client about the amount of energy needed.

Being Self-Employed – the Two Sarah's
Sarah has run her own company for over fifteen years now. She is a qualified interior designer and has worked for clients all over Ireland. During the boom times, she opened a shop in her native Cork, and for a time she also had a second shop in Limerick. While the recession years were tough, her good reputation and excellent client list saw her through, although she did let the shops go as they were making a loss that she couldn't sustain.

However, Sarah is getting tired of the uncertainty around being self-employed. The constant not knowing where the next work is coming from is proving to be a burden and she feels she needs more security in her life now. She feels like many entrepreneurs that she would just like to have a job that would pay her a salary, so she could leave the stress of running a business behind when she closes the door at home in the evening.

'But who would employ me?' She asks. 'Am I employable, having run a business for so long? Am I too old now to be starting out all over again?'

In order to self-actualise Sarah may need less working stimulus and more free time to concentrate on her inner search. These are questions I hear time and time again.

Crossing the bridge in the other direction is another Sarah, dying to let her entrepreneur out. She has been working in admin for the HSE for a number of years. The work is okay, but she could do without the pettiness and the office politics. This Sarah has always loved animals. Two years ago she trained as a dog groomer, and she has been working away doing a little on a part-time basis since then.

She loves every minute of it. Her clients love her too, they all say she has a gift for working with animals, and she should be doing this full-time. Sarah would love nothing better, but then there's the money. The HSE job gives nothing on the job satisfaction front, but the money is good. She knows she can rely on it. Here is the dilemma with which I am often confronted:

Is Sarah prepared to trade the security of the steady job, her absolute lack of fulfilment, for the joy of running her own business, the life she feels is in total alignment with her authentic self? Only she can decide but a consultation process assists to break it down into realisable goals, so it is not a reckless venture, but one that is fully enterprising.

If this Sarah wants to get on, she will work tirelessly, promoting and growing her passion. That is the magic ingredient of an entrepreneur. Proper research, business planning and then stepping into following a passion tirelessly, not being put off by inevitable setbacks, this focused approach will get you ninety-nine percent of the way there.

Not every enterprising individual wants to step out on their own. Some see the future in an organisation, but it has to see theirs.

'I Want to Get On.'

Jack is working for a large US Multinational. Recently he went for a promotion but was unsuccessful. Jack is beginning to notice that his friends are moving on in their careers, and so, he is feeling a bit stuck. He is in his late twenties now, and as a qualified engineer, he thinks he should be earning more.

He has worked hard, particularly in the last year and has eased off on the partying, to concentrate on his career. His appraisals are always good, but it doesn't seem to count when he applies for more senior positions. He peppers me with questions such as

Is it the company and does he need to move?

Is it because his boss doesn't like him and is holding him back?

Does he need a Masters?

All these questions are reaching for progression. One thing he is sure about is that he feels he needs to earn more money. The only way he can hope to earn more is by climbing the corporate ladder into management. We need a plan.

In some cases, clients are finally ready to embrace change when the pressure of their existing work becomes too much to bear.

'I Can't Keep Doing what I'm Doing.'

'Hi Tommy, how can I help?'

After a brief pause, Tommy pours out all of the stress and emotion that he has been holding onto for some time. He hates his job. He doesn't feel like he can stick it out. Tommy is under way too much pressure. He has no encouragement and feels like a rat in a trap. Stress is killing him. Whether Tommy is a salesman or a debt collector, he can't stand the targets. They loom large like an imposition over him, affecting his performance.

Even when he hits them, he has the next month to worry about. Constant pressure to match and improve his performance once drove him, but now it is driving him mad.

He is not getting any younger and feels like something is going to give. The money is good, and he feels secure financially. That's why he can't let go easily. There are people relying on him. Standards to keep.

Deep down Tommy knew long before the call, if he keeps doing what he is doing now; he could be close to a breakdown. He's become tired of making a profit for others and wants something now with a little less pressure.

While sales and target related work is the example I'm using here, you could easily substitute this scenario for working long, unsociable hours or indeed physical demands on the body.

Tommy needs structure now, and a plan to take him through to the next stage. Tommy needs his life back. But Tommy is clever. He knows he can study. He was good at it once. The next individual cannot remember what it felt like to sit an exam.

116

Dismissed as a young learner, he dismissed himself and took his prowess to the sports field where it got him noticed.

I left School behind Me

Adam had no motivation for school; he was easily distracted and spent most of his class time thinking of GAA and girls. The day he finished his Leaving Cert, he burned his uniform and thanked his lucky stars that it was all over.

Now, ten years later he is having major regrets and feels he left school behind.

He is recently married, and his wife is a qualified teacher. She is constantly egging him on to go back and get a degree, as she feels he is very unhappy and has lots of ability. But Adam feels bewildered by all of the jargon:

What's a graduate?
Am I too old for CAO?
Do I have to go back to full-time education?
How much will it all cost?
I haven't the slightest idea of what I want to do!

It's going to be a long session, but it will be a very productive one. I will help illuminate the college and qualification scene for Adam. It will be up to him and me to help him to see the light at the end of his career tunnel. I give the guidance; he does the work. We make the change together.

It might even bring up the same spirit that made him good in a game. He might be a forge-ahead entrepreneur scoring on an idea the way he once did goals on a sports field.

While your situation may not fit into any one of the above scenarios, there are many, many reasons why people seek to change or improve their career. In nearly all cases, it begins with a feeling of unease and uncertainty, or maybe just plain boredom.

When this happens, it is normally a sign that your inner motivational compass is pointing you to look at change and the possibilities that this may contain for you.

Facing change can bring on the feeling of fear, and sometimes the fear feeling might be so strong that you may be immobilised, and become paralysed with self-doubt. This can be more common in females than in males, but we all feel it to some extent. The trick is to persevere and get help. I have faced these fears before, and know how to overcome them.

A Career's Assessment?

There is nothing to worry about when it comes to having a session with a trained careers advisor. The process is simple, and we always start to look forward by looking back. We take stock of all your work and life experience to date, and in doing so, we identify the key transferable skills that you may bring to your new career.

Having teased this out with you, we then normally do a short gap analysis. I used to love strategic gap analysis thinking in my former company. Companies do this all of the time.

The approach is simple: this is where we are now, and this is where we want to be in the future. Companies then identify a list of key actions that they need to take, in order to close this gap. It's the same for you, what steps do you need to take to close the gap and realise your future self.

This part of the process is always real world and is grounded in reality. We take into consideration your current situation, and commitments and strive to find a plan for you that suits.

For example, if returning to education on a full-time basis is not possible, then we need to find alternative routes through part-time or possibly distance learning.

The process is never about pushing you to take steps that you are not ready for. Again, when I think of strategic planning, we always break our goals down into short-term, medium-term and long-term. But I urge you if you have the motivation, if you feel the need to self-actualize, start that process now.

I believe there is an amazing future awaiting you. You just have to track it using your own inner compass. No other one will do the right or same job. You have a destiny to fulfil.

7

THE FULLY ACTUALIZED ADULT

Chapter 7

Destiny's Child

The Fully Actualized Adult

'Do not go where the path may lead. Go instead where there is no path and leave a trail.'
Ralph Waldo Emerson

We are all greater than we imagine and also supported more than we think. Some people have a strong sense of destiny and believe that certain events were preordained or scripted and that these events would play a significant role in their own personal development. In my own experience, I was aware at times that certain forces beyond what can normally be sensed were definitely at play in shaping my own path. We hear of examples of this, all of the time.

My sister Nuala tells me that at one stage all she wanted to do was to become a Greenpeace volunteer. She sent her letter of application to Greenpeace headquarters in Geneva at the time and fully expected to be away in the Southern Ocean, saving the whales or preventing some nuclear tests soon after. But, she never heard anything from Greenpeace, as the saying goes, *not a dicky bird*. And so, she thought that maybe it wasn't for her. Fast forward to three years later, and a letter arrived unexpectedly from Greenpeace to Nuala.

Apparently, during an office move, a staff member discovered an unopened letter addressed to their recruitment office. When he opened and read it, he noticed the date. This letter had been sent three years previously, and he could only assume that somehow her letter of application must have fallen between cracks and lay there unopened for a full three years.

Greenpeace left the door open for Nuala to join them at that stage, but by then things had changed in her life. Destiny had called in another direction, and she answered it fully. She had opened a health store and healing centre in her hometown. It was going well, and she wanted to stay with the project and see it develop. And develop it did, into one of the largest health stores in the country. Through this centre and all its ancillary services, Nuala has helped thousands of people achieve a better quality of life.

It's a beacon in her hometown and attracts practitioners and clients from all over the region through its reputation. Was it meant to be? Probably! And, who knows, if she had gone to Greenpeace in the first instance, it might never have happened.

I always try to get my clients aligned with their higher selves and to get in touch with the flow of the Universe within them. I think there are always signs and clues that are given to us regarding what we need to do next.

Sometimes these clues can come from unexpected places.

I remember once a number of years ago I was at a psychic fair with a friend of mine and I met a lady who was doing free card readings. She offered one to me and during it told me she got a very strong sense of the media around me. Never in a thousand years did I see myself ever having any media involvement, but the power of suggestion is a strong one and seeing as she suggested it I decided to take a closer look.

And so a short while later I contacted my local radio station, South East Radio, and asked them if they would be interested in running some career guidance advice slots on their mid-morning programme. The answer was yes, and before I knew it, I was sitting at the microphone in the studio! It was the start of a very successful partnership, and I was happy to become South East Radio's career correspondent.

Again I have to ask the question I ask of my own sister's life path. Was this meant to be? I don't know. But the suggestion turned into a decision, and the opportunity presented, and it worked for all concerned – for the station, the presenter, the correspondent and those listening. There was a great ripple effect. There was a powerful effect. I overcame a natural reticence on my part to promote myself, to speak with experience and conviction on the topic I am qualified for and care about most. Career advice, life and spirit coaching, these are not just concerns for me. They are vocations.

Sometimes, when I am in the office with an uncertain person who has to find a future for themselves, and I am supporting that future through listening and input, I understand the greater power in my work is that I am not just working with this life, but the lives of those who the client encounters. This is the power of suggestion, prompted by the call of destiny and sustained by the belief and effort of the individual making their changes.

How could I not feel privileged? Even on difficult days, I see opportunities to make steps towards destiny. Sometimes the steps accelerate, other times it's hard to put one foot in front of the other.

But always destiny waits, and you are its child. Always, there is the possibility of becoming a fully actualized being.

Be alert to all possibilities in your life. Sometimes those we are close to, knowing us better than we do and can show us things about us that we can't see ourselves. Listen to your loved ones when they urge you to make changes. Don't be afraid of failures. They are places to learn from.

Getting it Wrong

Sometimes, it can be tricky deciding which hunches are worth acting on and which are not. I don't always get it right. Back in 2012, I had a feeling that I should develop a programme for Leaving Cert students who were preparing to go to college for the first time. I had asked a few parents and friends and most seemed to think it was a good idea. I thought it would be of great benefit to these students and also it would generate some cash for my business at a time that was traditionally quiet.

Following hours and hours of research, meetings and content development, I produced an outline for the programme and got a lovely colour brochure printed. The course was to be run in late July - early August when students were off, and I had everything in place and ready to go. I released the brochure to 150 clients that had attended for consultation, and I sat back and waited for the phone to ring. It was a long wait!

Of 150 potential candidates for the course, I received one reply. I was gobsmacked, and to be honest, my ego was taking a bit of a battering also. I could not understand why something that felt so good could go so badly wrong. Also, I was left with the prospect of having no work for this period during the summer.

But then, something really strange happened. A local medical device company rang me and asked me if I was available to do some staff training.

'How many?' I asked.

'All 250 of our staff,' was the answer.

This was technical, regulatory training. The company knew I had a background in technical and quality management and felt I was the man to do the job. After a couple of short meetings, we were ready to go. Not only did it fill my summer months to capacity, but I also had to take on additional staff to help with training delivery.

Was there a lesson to be learned? There was massive learning for me in this situation. The college preparation course had taken a huge effort from me to put it all together, and it was a complete flop. Yet in the case of the company training, it took just one phone call, and all the work I needed came flooding in with no effort on my part.

From that day on, I resolved to say goodbye to the old strategy of me dreaming up new possibilities and chasing ideas down blind alleys. From that day until the present moment I now allow work to come to me and I've never been disappointed. I call this process *alignment,* and I find this natural and easy. There is, of course, a certain level of trust needed, and at times it may seem like there's no notable work on the way. But thankfully this approach has worked really well for me and resulted in a great deal less stress in my life.

Hopefully, you can use this process of alignment in your life. Whenever you are feeling you are making very little progress and one door after another keeps closing, well maybe what you are trying so hard to achieve is not meant to be. This feels like paddling upstream against a strong current, lots of effort for very little gain. Work, and indeed life, shouldn't be like that. It's so much easier to allow the current take you down-stream and see where the destiny may take you.

A similar approach may be very useful in searching for your ideal career. So many times, I have pointed out at my seminars, that the problem for most people is not getting what they want but *not knowing what they want*. My experience of working with people has shown me that when they decide to pursue a particular goal/career, there is no holding them back and they will stop at nothing to achieve it.

Sean – Back to his Future

I first started work with Sean when he turned his back, through choice and chance, on a high profile position, and took a step into his inner direction and future. The reason was that he had never once in all his time of earning strong five-figure salaries and producing an award-winning product, had the sense that he had any right to be there. In fact, he hated it for most of the full decade; he worked at it. His CV had six job changes, each one promotion. He was a young tiger clawing his way to the top, or he was running from one.

Sean's destiny was a lot quieter than his talent had attracted.

'When I was younger, I won a big competition at school, and my father said that it was a sign I should work at it until it became a job. I listened to him because he was the most important influence of my working life. He had his whole family to support at the age of 14, and he had survived the major recessions by negotiating the line between work fulfilment and family duty. The family won each time, and he did jobs way below his ability and put his all into his family. He was my hero.

'But he did set me on the wrong path, thinking it was the right one.'

Things improve with every generation, and Sean's father had battled not just as an adult but as a child to earn a living. He learned how to do that, and he learned quickly. He had a huge intellect and a limited circumstance. So destiny called on him to compromise his own dreams and be a strong link in the ancestral chain, creating chances for his children he could never hope for.

The difference between a hope and a dream is a dream stays in and is harboured, while hope is the feeling you wake up with and carry on. The dream might be your destiny, but the hope is the fuel to achieve it. In the same way, my sister Nuala thought her destiny was Greenpeace, it was green, but a more local campaign to improve life and circumstance for local warriors battling health issues and those who wanted to maintain full health.

Sean's job was the kind that sends customers to my sister's health shop for remedies for stress relief. Just because you are good at something, you don't have to do it for a living. Sean trusted his father's heroism so much he bet his future on his father's advice and his own instinct was shocked to find, at college, studying what his father had a thwarted passion for; he had not a full feeling of destiny or arrival at a true calling. In fact, he hated his classmates. They were tough and self-directed ready to push for careers in technology and innovation with big returns for endless hours.

You have to consider your own personality when making choices, and Sean's was, if I am honest, a lot more sensitive than his father. He was also more suited to the pursuit of his own desires than to a dream of the last generation. His father could have become a strong contender in business but ended up in a trade to get the money rolling in the door quicker.

Time and again I am told money has been the deciding facture in overruling the call of destiny. What people fail to realise is that proper planning towards destiny, using the process of consultation and the planning of critical paths, will create the opportunities. In short don't be afraid to change. Be afraid of not changing if you know you're not going in the direction you were meant to. Don't be afraid of failure. Be afraid of avoiding failure to stay somewhere you hate working.

Consider yourself, and you will find yourself. Work hard at your hunches and clean the egg from your face when the hunch cracks and splatters. Persevere if you still, after inevitable setbacks, feel drawn to the desire you had hoped for. Destiny is a child not just of indications, but of whether you are prepared to follow those indications.

Sean, at twenty-seven, had had a short and frightening illness that helped him put things into consideration.

'I spent about six months having treatment that put everything into perspective. I was in a long-term relationship, but we had no children. I could see this was my last chance. The illness gave me an opportunity to get off the wheel and change my fortune.'

The thing most people think is when they come to my office destiny will change for them. It simply doesn't operate like this. A consultation is the first step in a process that will involve consideration and perspiration. The right moment to change is when you're ready to work on it.

Sean decided he couldn't cope with the cut and thrust of the top echelons of his business environment and he was one step away from being placed in it.

'I was great at my last job, so my ability got me noticed, but my heart wasn't in it. I've a strong work ethic, and it possibly worked against me. I just got things over the line and didn't take consideration of myself. The illness was, without doubt, a shock, but I was going to be promoted and stay where I was without question.'

During his six-month treatment, he worried sick for two months about getting back to work before he lost his job; the next two months were spent stressing about how he would cope when he got back and the last two months were spent planning to take his new direction.

'Suddenly life was more important. I felt sick at the thought of returning to what might even make me sick again.'

The last two months put him in my office, and he figured out where he sat archetypally and what his needs were. His cognitive needs were met by work and the high challenge of his job, in a company providing multimedia content. It all tore at his downtime, so he didn't reflect. But self-actualization was not even approaching consideration prior to this.

'Twenty-six weeks of non-stop thinking and I couldn't understand how I got to twenty-seven without thinking for myself.'

I am not a therapist, and I put this across straight away when it looks like a client has emotional difficulties beyond their job. Sean began to work with a counsellor, and the sessions with her showed him that profound admiration for his father was well deserved, but not serving him well in terms of his own identity. Sean is the kind of man that if he knows what the problem is he will do his utmost to fix it.

Still, he was reduced to an age of single digits in confronting his dad, who spoke about his son's achievements at every available opportunity. I could help with this one by asking:

'If you are successful as something you're not suited to, imagine the impact you'll make on a role that you are more matched with.'

This swung it. He arranged to tell his parents his intention was not to resume the position being kept open for him. But he was going to find work before resigning, to make things right. Also, he had not fully recovered, that took another six months. If he had gone back to work fulltime at that stage, his relapse might have taken years instead of just one.

'I told my father that if he had been in business, he might have earned a million, but he was one in a million as a father. He saw his own regret for his own life in a different way. The failure he felt was a success in getting one of his own children the chances he would have loved. That was one of the best nights of my life sitting down with him to sort it out.'

In the months after the meeting, his father had to adjust to what the support meant, and a few rows took place. But Sean held to his course, as his destiny was his chief concern.

'No one likes to disappoint their parents and particularly when you have ones like mine. They loved to tell stories about my shooting up the ladder, and they saw I would be a partner before I was thirty.'

What Sean's parents had to adjust to, Sean also had to adjust to. He was not going to be a high flier; he was not going to continue to earn his weight in bonuses and high salaries. He was not suited temperamentally or physically to high-stress environments.

'Years before anyone said a word to me about what I would be when I grew up; I said working with people. I met a lot of people in my old role and the way I met them, in tough negotiations, was putting me off human nature.'

Change can cause great turbulence. Who you are might make others happy, but you have to live your own story. The ricochet of leaving a prime position, the previous six months where he had not worked or earned money, now also not being able to enjoy trips and breaks as much as he had done before, put a strain on his marriage.

As part of his illness, Sean had the double whammy of his marriage ending as he came out of it.

'It was definitely the right decision. We were a great support to each other when we both worked so hard. She thrives on her job in management, and I was a great listener to her issues with it. Her advice to me was that I had lost my confidence being out of work and facing my health challenge. I'd be alright when I got back to it.'

'One night she turned to me and asked me straight out if I wasn't happy the way things were before I got sick. I told her that I was, but that I couldn't stay with the way things were when I was well. I wanted a change. I'm turning thirty soon, and I'm so different to what I was when I met her.'

As an interim change, while he pursues his ultimate goal, we determined that he was suited to consultation. Within a few months of applying for positions, Sean got his first job in a development role that assists people who want to break into the industry he just left full-time. He also teaches in the evenings and weekends. Even though he has a job and a half, he still has more time to himself than he has ever had.

'The salary is a lot less. Time is more precious than money. In fact, it's priceless.'

Getting his life back is putting his life forward. Taking less money is getting him a more personal life. Sean will begin his new project in the next year and when he puts all that energy he once used for others into himself, he will be someone who reaches his ultimate destiny.

While you would never wish what he has been through, on him, his determination to dig deep and make his destiny come to him has brought the best results. There is more to come. He has a lot more to do and a lot more to be.

Drilling for Destiny

'To find water, you do not dig many shallow holes all over the place. You drill deep in one place only.'
Sri N. Maharaj

Wise words indeed! When drilling go deep, when we are digging deep, we discard all the material that is of no use to us, until we uncover what we are looking for. When future options are not clear, people need to drill, take the time and reflect on what may or may not suit their needs values and circumstances.

It can help to have the support of a trained careers adviser during this process, but if you can't avail of this support for whatever reason, it can be done on your own.

This step mostly needs a combination of quiet space and time.

Like Sean, sometimes a person may experience an illness and have been forced to take time out; they often make subsequent changes in their lives for the better. How often have you heard people say:

'I decided there and then that my life needed to change and that if I recovered from my illness, I was going to make those changes.'

For others, they might take a holiday or go on a retreat to literally find themselves. Nowadays, it is very popular to walk the Camino de Santiago, which stretches from the south of France to the North West corner of Spain, in the hope that the pilgrimage might be the catalyst for change. This is not always necessary, and sometimes there is no need for such extreme measures or actions.

You can walk your own Camino!

In my case, it was a wet Sunday, one of those Sundays where you look out the window and watch rain roll by in giant wind-driven sheets. I was at home. At that time, I had been thinking about my next career move but wasn't making much progress. With nothing coming to me there and then, I decided to take some time out and have a nap lying on the floor as I was accustomed to. For some reason, it wouldn't happen. With no sleep coming I focused in on my future direction. What came to me made no immediate sense, but would make perfect sense a short while later.

I saw in my mind a clear picture of a chair. But not any old chair. It was a big leather chair with stud buttons and large winged armrests. I found out later that they are called Winchester chairs. It didn't make any sense. But it was the first symbol of my impending business start-up. The image fired up the synapses and questions came at me. Why this leather chair? It was actually more of a *who* than a *why*.

'Who normally uses these chairs?' I asked myself.

Traditionally I would have associated these with doctors or lawyers.

'What do they have in common?' I asked out loud.
Giving advice.
But, I didn't feel qualified to give anybody advice.
'What could I be giving people advice on?' I asked.

I kept thinking about the chair, and how I might use the inspiration. At the time, I was working in Human Resource Management and had come to know a lot about CV's, interviews, job applications and careers in general. There was the match! I could give people advice on a range of human resource, employee and career training issues.

But, was there a market? Absolutely! There were very few people offering a service in this area. I felt ready to run with the idea and in no time was getting ready to start up my own business. To this day I still don't know where the image of the leather chair came from, but I know it was the right one and that it was definitely meant for me.

This led to one step, which led to hundreds more and now leads me writing this book for you. There are hundreds if not thousands of books out there at the moment to help you find your true purpose, but you may not need them. You might just need to take some time. Sometimes, ideas relating to inspiring futures can't reach us, simply because our minds are far too busy with chatter to let them in.

Have you noticed lately that for lots of people it's not enough anymore to be just watching TV? They have a second technology device on the go. We have created a very complicated world.

In my view, a lot of this activity is meaningless and designed to keep us from looking at how we actually feel about ourselves. If we looked at these feelings, we would probably realise how unhappy we are, and we might have to make changes in our lives. So we employ distractions to divert our attention away.

But the message will reach us somehow to signify that we have to allow change to occur. If we allow stillness and solitude, we will be self-directed far quicker than if we avoid the mechanism of change which tends to use frustration at current circumstance as its starting point.

It's okay to feel frustration; it's not okay to be frustrated all the time and not try to change whatever is not right.

Without all this frantic mind activity, we just might have a chance of seeing our future possibilities through an untarnished lens. In doing so, we can create a better future for ourselves and for others. So go on, have a go.

Take some time out to reflect on what it is you want to do with the rest of your life. The longer you put it off, the harder it will become. There's a huge world out there to be experienced, and I promise you will never regret embracing change and starting out on your own personal journey of self-discovery.

8

THE VOICELESS VOICE

Chapter 8

The Voiceless Voice

Decisions and their Making

'There is a voice that doesn't use words. Listen.'
Rumi

 Decisions - we make them all of the time. From daily to lifetime choices, we are constantly faced with them. The truth is if we are aware enough we will always trust the voiceless voice, the one inside who has something to say about all our events, intuitions, opportunities, questions and dilemmas.

If we spend time with it, we will discover quickly that the voiceless voice is not silent. It is just the one that no one else can hear. It is our individual, internal and unique dialogue and it is the voice of change. It will speak up during every decision process, but sometimes, because we are wary of trusting ourselves fully, we will say we don't know what we want to do, that we cannot hear our intuition. That we simply cannot decide. It might even come down to the tossing of a coin, seriously, more on this later.

'I'm not good at making decisions,' the client who tells me this is telling me that they have forgotten, for now, to listen to themselves. It doesn't take all that long to remind them that from babyhood to adulthood no day is without making some decision or other. But at times when we have to make a big, conscious choice such as what we are going to work at, we can forget we ever made one at all.

At some point in the career guidance process, decisions need to be taken. Some people find making these decisions very difficult and challenging, and in a lot of cases, they actually want me to take this step for them. Of course, this is something I can't and am not prepared to do. However, it is worth exploring this particular dilemma, one that so many people face.

The root of the word *decide*, means to slay as in *homicide*, or *suicide*. One of the reasons we find deciding for something so hard, is because invariably, in doing so we are killing other options. It's worth noting that one of the most quoted poems in the world, *The Road Not Taken* by Robert Frost, from which Scott Peck's self-development classic *The Road Less Travelled* takes its title, is often quoted by the title Peck used, but the implication of the derived title is different to the original one.

The poem, while it acknowledges in the last lines the poet's decision to take a less travelled road, does not just concentrate on this, it examines the regret of leaving one choice behind opening with these two lines:

Two roads diverged in a yellow wood,
And sorry I could not travel both.

Frost laments and presses on the path that was meant for him. He did not emerge as a poet until he was a family man in his forties. It made all the difference to poetry lovers and deep thinkers that he focused on the choice, and took the one that was difficult for him. He came up with the emblem for life itself. But it is this very thing, this sense that our entire life is being held up for question, in our desire and intention to follow our true selves, and fashion a career path, that makes guidance so necessary and so initially frightening.

At times, we may not be quite ready to do so. But if we want to be happy we have to make efforts to make ourselves as fulfilled by work as possible.

Now, let's move on to some other lines that reflect career guidance as work to help people make decisions that will inform and change not just their working lives, but their entire existence:

And be one traveler, long I stood
And looked down one as far as I could
To where it bent in the undergrowth;

We begin with the realisation, straight away that all change involves loss – you have to let go of something to gain new ground. Often it is this very fear that puts people in the chair beside mine. I never sit behind a desk with people. It is about us travelling their road together for as long as they want to or need consultation.

The prevarication is the first precipice. The options overwhelm, the decisions threaten as well as liberate. It's hard and important work to develop. No wonder so many clients want me to make their decisions for them! I don't blame them and would have done the same when I was in my late teens, as I did with my father when he drove me to the Carlow Institute of Technology to study something I had no clear aptitude for or interest in.

According to the famous psychiatrist Irvin D. Yalom's book *'Love's Executioner*, for every *yes* there must be a corresponding *no* for each decision, thus killing or eliminating other possibilities. We see this at play all of the time, from the smallest decision, of what to order off a menu, to one of our common and most important decisions, getting married.

While the prospect of having a partner for life can be very comforting, the impending and subsequent loss of our personal freedom can seem quite foreboding. In relationships, this can often manifest as lack of commitment. It is precisely this reluctance that Yalom talks about, arising from the death of the possibility of continuing personal freedom.

Frost's poem encapsulates this process further when he goes on to write about his desire to return and take the other road sometime:

Yet knowing how way leads on to way,
I doubted if I should ever come back.

Chapter 8 – The Voiceless Voice

Even when our clocks go back this is a deception – time always moves forward. We have to face that we have shut down the avenues that might have been when we press on. So it is so important in our working lives to take the road we wish to take, as way does lead to way and a role we are not suited to can lead us away from ourselves.

A job is a marriage of you to your means of supporting yourself. No wonder changing it can feel overwhelming. Although clients generally are not prepared to admit to their absolute terror in deciding one way or the other, it is very often the sole reason they come to see me. Decisions have to be made.

Frost took his:

'I shall be telling this with a sigh
Somewhere ages and ages hence:
Two roads diverged in a wood, and I—
I took the one less traveled [SIC] by,
And that has made all the difference.'

One of my good friends has no trouble deciding to splash out significant amounts on a new car. But if you ask him where he wants to go to lunch he struggles to make his mind up. Why does such a big spender fear the outcome of a choice between a Chinese or Italian? It is indicative of something. Oftentimes the big deciders, those who risk and push as a given in their careers can feel like a little child in the other areas. We can be good at anything we set our mind to, but we cannot be good at everything.

During World War Two, the RAF needed decisive people to train as fighter pilots, capable of making snap decisions in highly pressurised situations. Yet commercial airlines found that this type of gung-ho personality was completely unsuitable for flying passenger aircraft in peacetime, and was indeed the cause of many air accidents.

Big risk takers have vulnerable sides, manifested in a dilemma over black bean sauce or cannelloni. People who pay great attention to detail and order can struggle over the intuitive aspects. Consultation is the other side of the see-saw - balancing your vulnerabilities, pointing out your strengths. Helping you adjust to the changes, the losses and find the new equilibrium.

A client of 40 will differ to a client of 20 years of age. The older ones have already figured out that decisions don't become any less frightening, we just get more used to dealing with the fears involved.

A Lesson in Decision Making

Experience teaches us so much. My own definition of experience is someone who has made that mistake before (and learned from it). My former boss Tony Donegan taught me my most valuable lesson in decision-making. At the time I was managing a small team of skilled technicians. One of these technicians was needed by our U. S. plant in California. It would be an all-expenses-paid trip to sunny San Francisco for one of the guys, but the trouble was, which one?

At the time there were two very capable and deserving candidates, and understandably both had expressed a strong interest in going. The final call on who travelled was totally up to me, and I was having real difficulty in making the decision. I couldn't face telling one of those hard working chaps that he wasn't selected. I mulled over it for days.

Finally, when I couldn't stand it any longer, I went into Tony's office and told him my dilemma.

'I can't make up my mind Tony,' I remember saying. 'Whoever doesn't get to go to the U. S. is going to be very unhappy.'

'Seamus my good man,' he answered. 'You had better make your mind up quickly. One of the guys is going to have his nose out of joint, but right now there are three people very unhappy. Both technicians are unhappy because you are leaving them hanging in a state of uncertainty, and you are unhappy because you can't make the damned decision. So go and make your decision, let them know, and then we can all move on.'

The penny dropped. I quickly communicated my decision based on what I thought was the right criteria. The news was taken well by all parties. Interestingly a short while later another request was made for one of our technicians to travel, this time to South

America, and I was delighted to be able to offer it to the technician who didn't get the first trip.

Sometimes we can't get everything we want from a decision. But the misery caused by not deciding is far greater. That situation provided a great lesson for me, and it is learning that I use, to help my indecisive clients on a regular basis.

Emma – in need of Persuasion

Consider the case of Emma, a Leaving Cert student who comes for assessment. In her introduction, Emma tells me she has no idea what she wants to do. Then she generates a long list of potential careers, most of which she is either unsuitable for or has no real intention of doing. But there is a theme in the machine gun fire of her process. She has two strong options which she continually refers to. They hit the target each time.

Most of her questions come down to the two careers she asks most about. She also seems to have researched these in depth. We make our way through the short-listing process, and - lo and behold - it's the same two careers that make it to her final list.

For anybody familiar with the CAO process, they will know that it is absolutely essential that Emma places her top two choices in order of preference. When confronted with the moment of commitment to either one of her top two, there is a pause. Emma can't decide. Her body language and demeanour change. She gets visibly nervous and agitated, won't make eye contact and when she does, perspiration glistens on her forehead.

Finally, she asks if can we go over these two careers again and she asks all of the same questions. Its decision time, and she can't make it.

Rather than being angry or frustrated at her being stuck and retreating back over old ground, I feel sorry for Emma who is just turning eighteen and has all of this responsibility on her young shoulders.

How unfair. Emma is not so much afraid of the decision, but how it will affect the rest of her life.

Will she be suited to her instinctive choices?
Will she get the grades she needs to secure them?

What if she is taking the wrong road?

The choices she is depriving herself of, in making her top two selections, is where her centre of gravity starts to spin. Is she on the wrong axis? What she needs most now is the reassurance that everything is fine. It's all going to work out well. She may also need a little coaxing.

At this point in my own mind, I am on the road to Carlow, trusting my father that he has found something I don't have a clue about. He is older than me, and he is wiser than me. But did he, at that age, know me better than I knew myself?

I can't put money on it, but I think at the time he was doing his best for his son and the best at the time was that it was better to be doing something than doing nothing.

You can't put an old head on young shoulders, but you can listen with older and wiser ears to what Emma truly wants. She doesn't need lectures of the *why can't you make your mind up* variety. Right now Emma needs concrete examples and a modicum of wisdom given through illustrations rather than dictates.

So I use my life as I've used it through the book, to point out my errors and the avenues opened up by learning from them. I tell her what I think about decisions myself. Here is what I have come to know about the process. There is no such thing as a right or a wrong decision; there are only circumstances.

Decision One brings in one set of circumstances. Decision Two brings a different set. What is key here is the person's ability to make the most of any given set of circumstances. It is so important that the client recognises this.

There is no need to worry about making a bad or wrong decision that is going to impact them for the rest of their life. Every time we walk through one door another door opens on our journey.

To help people at the decision-making stage, I ask them to dig deep and see how their *second brain* feels what is right for them to do. This is located right in their gut. Scientists have labelled this the *second brain* because it is so similar to the brain in terms of the neurological chemicals produced.

The system is called the enteric nervous system, and it has a direct connection to the brain via a long nerve called the vagus nerve. We also know that both systems are in constant communication with each other through this nerve. The second brain is much better known as your *gut feeling*. It is an intuitive force, and I call it the **voiceless voice**.

It is very developed in lots of people, probably more so in women than in men, and is often used as a protective mechanism, for example, when we get a strong sense of something not feeling right for us. And so, I appeal to my clients to get a feel of what course or career feels right for them.

Coin Spins for Head Spins

In some cases, I spin an imaginary coin in slow motion. During the process, I ask the client to think about which options they would like the coin spin to select for them. In nearly all cases, they choose the most suitable option and the option that "feels" right at that time. Although simple, this is a process that rarely if ever lets me down.

In this way, I help the person to help themselves. The voiceless voice speaks because there is an activity – the coin visualisation – and an opportunity - the consultation – combining to create the circumstances for a new direction.

The No Decision

One decision that seems much easier than *yes* is the *no* decision. It is very prevalent in young people. I regularly encounter Leaving Cert students, who are very clear regarding those careers that they *do not* want to do. Their responses to my questions are clear and direct:

'That's not for me. I hate science.'
'You must be joking. I've no patience with kids.'
'I've already looked at business. I've decided against it.'
'I'm squeamish when it comes to blood.'

In most cases, there is very little room for compromise. No means no. All of the no answers appear well thought out. These students can give me rational reasons for not choosing specific careers, but little indication as to what they might enjoy or secretly enjoy but are too afraid to say. They see me as the one finding the needle in their haystack. They feel that if I'm good at my job, I will somehow find their vocation on their behalf, and they won't have to put themselves into the choice.

If it does go wrong, it will be my fault. Not theirs. Again I feel a certain level of sympathy for them because the decision that might not be right is seen as something deemed out of their control and thus they are absolved of responsibility. In this situation, the career advisor's skills are pushed to the limit.

Apart from staying patient and open to clients, there is also the worry as to whether we will, in fact, find any career that has the magic dust of affirmation. In the end, this fear is worked through, mostly because the CAO deadline is looming. Faced with the prospect of having no offer from the postman on Offers day, the client becomes more open to positive outcomes.

Having eliminated most possibilities, they now retrace to find the few that might be where their future lies. This time they are selecting from a much smaller pool of careers. In the end, through perseverance, patience and prompting, we nearly always seem to find something. However, I do wonder if this strategy is just another ploy to avoid making clear-cut decisions?

In this scenario, it seems by ruling out greater than 95% of the options the client almost arrives by default at their choice and effectively has the decision made for them. I am still open to thinking that this is a decision by elimination. It seems to me that it would be easier if the voiceless voice was truly heard.

In her book *The Right Questions,* Debbie Ford gives you ten amazing questions to ask yourself in the moment of choice about future career choices, or broader life choices. I won't go into them all now, but I think the key focus is in listening to the voice of self over others.

Debbie's questions are structured in such a way to get you to think about your decisions (or lack of them) and how the results of these decisions will impact your future life. The questions are designed to help you reflect on issues such as short-term gratification versus long-term gain. In effect she forces us to look at those consequences that all decisions we make have, and whether or not we are being pro-active in our choices or just reacting to our societal conditioning and what others expect from us.

It all comes down to faith over fear. If you have faith in yourself, you will choose to support yourself in your choices. If you have more of a fear of failure and its outcomes, than belief in your instinct, you will make choices that reflect your fear.

Sometimes the river flows but nothing breathes.
A train arrives but never leaves.
It's a shame.
Search for the Hero (M People)

Fear, of course, is the underlying factor behind the inability and reluctance to make tough decisions. Fear is yet another strategy of the mind to keep us safe, but tragically there is a very high price to pay for the safety, that of complete immobilisation. Fear immobilises and wants to keep you stuck where you are right now. Change challenges us to grow and learn and has the opposite effect of maintaining the status quo.

When I think of Maslow et al., and all of their great theories, our nature is to evolve as a species and become the best that we can be. Staying stuck, of course, is the complete opposite, where we attempt to keep control over a world which is very impermanent and where everything moves on at a relentless pace.

Charles Handy, in his book *The Empty Raincoat* summed up his approach to life perfectly when he wrote:

'*I want to be all used up by the time I reach that time when my life will end. I want to be like an old piece of cloth – worn out and threadbare from all of its use. I want to leave nothing behind*'.

Central to Handy's approach, is a desire to seek out new learning opportunities and embrace change, and in doing so to experience as many diverse life experiences as possible.

Live your changes. Learn from your failures. Build on your successes.

Listen to your voiceless voice. In time it will be one you hear most clearly and the one you learn most from. Brian's life is evidence of this.

The Life of Brian

One of the things I have had to accept early on with clients is that a decision is made as much out of instinct as an opportunity. A client can have all the right ingredients to follow a certain path, but the prospect is never as revealing as the reality. In terms of those who carry the sword all the way through the battle, then put it down even though it's theirs, I can only say – trust and follow your own direction.

Several examples of those who have gone through the blood sweat tears and trials of a primary degree, only to find that it wasn't their primary ambition, come to mind. But nothing is ever wasted. All learning is progression and progress is made in every choice we make.

Brian's life is a case; it followed a steep incline and levelled out on the ridge he was made for. A fairly typical teenager, he was good at sports and, while he had lots of academic ability, he wasn't very motivated about studying. Despite the fact he preferred an active lifestyle; he also had a head for figures and opportunities. His communication skills were strong. So he put it all together and came up with the prospect of teaching.

As I have said in the assessment chapter this is what makes testing a person only a part of the evaluation, but not an entirety. On paper, Brian had the ingredients. In person, he had a life story larger than the possibility he put in front of him as a career. Maybe it was the holidays, perhaps the social aspect, but despite the fact he found academic aspects of school low on his agenda, his chosen career at the time was secondary teaching. His mother was a secondary teacher, and she was a good role model for him.

He decided on doing business studies, chose two business subjects in the Leaving Cert, got the points he needed and headed off to college. The paper trail again was good, but the trials were beginning to line up.

All seemed well in the first year, and although he had a couple of repeat exams at the end of the first year, he successfully negotiated those and progressed into the second year. In the second year Brian seemed to question his course choice. As he was bright, he had managed at school to keep engaged enough to get through. A degree course demanded more of his attention and his capabilities to complete were being called into question.

Brian just was not being Brian. The multiple choice pattern of his life was not suited to a linear, steadfast approach. He liked to engage; he liked activity. There was simply too much sitting down to a business degree to suit his profile and personality. At the time a combination of factors seemed to be contributing to his doubts and possibly having a busy social life was one of those. But the active side of him, the energiser, was rising and demanding to be heard and participate in his choices.

In addition, he was finding economics tough, like many business students, and struggled to get the required grades to move him into the third year. Again, following a number of repeats he managed to scrape through to the third year. It just wasn't coming so easily. It wasn't coming at all.

The express train that change becomes if instinct is not listened to and regarded, came hurtling for him and he was tied to the tracks of having put effort into something he was not truly aligned to. He had roped himself down. In his third year of the course, things came to a head. Brian had to face up to the reality that teaching business was no longer a career option that he wanted to pursue.

The final year of a degree is a hard and lonely time to leave a course at. While his entire cohort had the ticker tape in sight, he was left with an empty reality. The only thing pulling him out of the race was the cry of his own surety, together with the on-paper results to prove his discontent. You can't put square pegs in round holes when they're too big for the hole in the first place.

So, thousands of hours and money invested and nothing to show for it, he joined the long line of students that leave a course before they finish and then had to face the inevitable question of what to do next. This is the kind of vacuum people can lose a decade in. They feel the immediate relief of getting off the treadmill and the immediate panic that there is nothing out there for someone who doesn't know what they want to do next.

Get a job. Any job! Put money where the uncertainty is. The more you can save at this key stage, the easier it will be to find the next direction. It also gives the days that can be overwhelming a structure. Brian took a job in retail and began to ponder what the future held for him. Then it came to him. His passion had been for the active life and sport of any kind. He then decided to focus in on sports having had enough knocks to know that treating injuries has become big business now that people take care of the bodies they exercise. A short course in the management of sports injuries showed him that his positive, outgoing nature wasn't keen on listening to a litany of complaints about ligaments. Another year on the clock and he decided that treating sports injuries wasn't exactly what he was looking for.

Brian's nature was direct, positive and productive. He didn't care for academia, but he had a natural interest in experiential learning. As he had gone along the road of business, picking up sports theory, he found his interest in nutrition growing and sports nutrition was advised by a relative.

A part-time course in Dublin which would qualify him as a nutritional therapist fitted the bill. His picture began to form. His instinct was growing that he was getting closer to his real earning and living potential. He found the application he had lacked in earlier learning instances because he was engaged with the subject that suited. The focus was no longer a problem; it was brought to study the same way he had brought it to the sports and social parts of his life. So, while continuing to work, he studied hard and managed to gain a professional diploma. After three years he was now a qualified nutritional therapist.

Jobs in this area followed. His first major break was the management of a major health store in Dublin city centre, a brief stint as a sales representative with a major nutritional brand showed him just what possibilities, and customers, the world of supplements offers. Three years working in the area of nutrition and health, and at age 28, he was approaching an area in his life where he was looking for future development.

We are living longer, and so bodies need to last longer. The products were not keeping pace with the growing and complex needs of a population who are hungry to be healthy. He decided to take a review of the whole health and nutrition market, the products and services that were being provided, and more importantly, those that were not.

One area that seemed to have been neglected was the whole area of nutritional support for couples who were experiencing issues around fertility. What Brian found was that there was a range of what he thought were poorly designed products and that these were often highly priced. The price reflected the desperation of couples, and in his research, he heard enough stories to make him realise that more of them would benefit from supplementation that pinpointed their specific needs. He decided to focus in on this whole area of nutritional supplement support, for couples who were aiming to conceive and developed a formulation which met all of the regulatory requirements.

Designing a nutritional product such as this was only the first step.

Brian was faced with the major challenge of how to bring this product to the market. A question I am often asked at this stage is: 'Do I need a business degree in order to start my own business?' And the answer, as you know, is always 'No'.

But Brian had the energy of an entrepreneur and the brain of a former business studies student who had almost lasted the entire degree course. He might not have had the piece of paper, but he did have prior learning. He also had the thing no entrepreneur can be deprived of – determination. Thankfully lots of support is available for budding entrepreneurs, and Brian was lucky enough to get in touch with his local County Enterprise Board (LEO) at the time.

They provided all of the help, training and support that he needed to bring his vision to the market. He turned his dream into a plan, spending the next year developing his website, promotional materials, marketing and PR. He worked with a number of approved manufacturers, to produce the high-quality product that he was looking for. The social side that had put paid to a life behind a desk or in a classroom thrived on networking, with his trademark optimism he attended many fares and conferences and presented his product to anybody who was prepared to listen.

The day the supplement launched he saw all his life history, his school difficulty, social inclination, bright mind, outgoing nature, determined vision and work ethic culminate in a box that might change the lives of people who needed it badly. A product with beneficial purposes is something most admire, but this man, a touch into his twenties was offering a cost-effective, more effective alternative to some of the most vulnerable consumers in the country. His product won many awards. He was also awarded, as one of Ireland's Best Young Entrepreneurs.

Had he known, back when the business degree and future employment prospects dwindled, that he would stand on a stage collecting a prize for something that came out of all his trials and errors, it might have made life easier. But his life has the meaning so many others who don't follow potential, lack. While the early years were tough, as they often are for new business start-ups, the product has really taken off over the past twelve months. It is currently doing very well in Ireland, the UK, the Middle-East and is soon to spread to other countries within the EU.

Brian started out with a business degree with the full intention of becoming a teacher, but the truth was he was an avoider, who had no idea what he wanted and thought teaching might teach him a thing or two. It taught him he wasn't one. But his life's work has taken on an instructional approach; he is of use, and all his errors were steep, slanting stones to step on. He did not complete his degree, but his early years in business did prove very beneficial.

I see this, time and again in my work with clients that have taken on a course of studies. My guidance of someone like Brian, in turn, gives my life and work meaning. I am helping a man find a direction out of his questions. I am helping him live his answer. In his field, he is doing the same. This is life-giving.

In many cases, the reason for having completed a course was not apparent at the time, but later in life studies such as these are nearly always put to good use. The life of Brian is a life worth examining to see how a tangent is sometimes not that at all, but an opportunity for truth. For some, not all, the convention of, 'a good job' is the real tangent.

The only thing Brian does these days is something he believes in. Do what you love, and you will not work a day in your life.

9

TURNING POINTS

Chapter 9

Turning Points

Finding your Fulcrum

Career guidance is helpful at the key stages in life as we discussed in a previous chapter. There is a strong sense from some clients that the work is carried out and reaches completion within the time frame of the session.

It does, but the sessions are a fulcrum or turning point at which decisions are made and then the work of the decisions made begins. All work is ongoing and this why the use of a good career guide can help make the shifts into each stage and answer the questions of your current life.

Probably one of the key reasons why the work feels more overwhelming in the early stages is life experience is still being built up. When I was smelling ammonia, there was a sense I would smell it forever if I didn't do something about it and I had to do it quickly. There was urgency and a degree of panic. Now I am in my contemplative sixties I see the question of my roaring twenties was – who am I? What I was going to do with my life was a part of this question but not all of it.

This chapter is for young adults who think if they do not make the right decision they have not made a decision at all. The only right decision is to take the next step and see where it leads you.

Once you have used the evaluative programme *Soon to Be Me* ™ and had a consultation, you will be ready to make moves. They will be the right move for that time, and that can change over time.

So I've chosen two key clients to illustrate how a career decision can also shed light on life, but not solve every dilemma of every life. The two people you are going to meet have had very different life experiences when it comes to education – one is a high achiever, the other a returner to learning – but they have the same determination and quality of thought that makes for a fully developed existence.

Right now, as they work with me, they are asking a lot of questions. The sense is one of turbulence for them by times, but I see their shared trait – determination – bringing them some rich and meaningful answers. They have realised a career is also about life purpose and so they are finding careers with meaning decades before others look for it. A job for these two people will not be about money alone – it will be about self-expression.

They are living their changes and facing their turning points with bravery. One is in her early thirties, the other in her early forties. Both have come through a trauma – one inflicted by a misguided teacher who failed to alleviate or understand the pressure she was putting on a high-achieving student; the other suffered childhood abuse and violation, and despite a start, most of us would describe as horrendous, has found the beauty in her own life and self. She is working with this to find a way of earning money that takes into account all of her personhood and allows her to use the kind of life-wisdom gained from suffering.

Meet Anna and Eva – both living their changes and realising that while they cannot answer all their questions, they are going to be the best they can be in the time and stage they are in.

Let's begin with Eva

There are soft scars on her arms, which signify a time when she could not carry on. She has had a beautiful, freeing tattoo placed on them and to say she is beautiful in all ways is not enough to describe her presence. When she arrives in my office, she is often anxious and within moments has let her true spirit into her moment.

The woman is a vision to look at, but it is her vision for herself, her sheer strength, to raise her daughter single-handedly, in a manner she herself could have only dreamed of, her bravery in allowing herself to be loved by a man who is good to her, that combine and conspire with her ongoing development in working life.

Each day this rare and exceptional being, who is slight, gets up to drive a bus around the small byroads and take people to places of work and education. She sat her LPSV licence and passed the second time when she was told by the love of her life just to trust herself. This is what she comes for career counselling for.

Pure love and instinct have created a path for Eva. It can't be done alone, but it can be done. Eva tells her story today with support. When she first needed to tell it, there was no one qualified to tell it through.

This slip of a woman slipped in behind the giant steering wheel and guided herself into the first part of her new working future. She had run her own business by the time she was thirty and bought her own home and raised her child while doing so. All of this was done with little formal qualification, but Eva is immensely well qualified for life and living.

Each day she makes the decision not to do what was done to her.

'I have had to make the decision to change the way I am rearing my daughter. It is the complete opposite to how I was reared. I am rearing her to be proud of who she is.'

She is passionate about her daughter, has found the passion in a fully supported relationship and is now finding the passion for herself.

This resolve caused her first to seek deep therapy, for her own trauma, then to progress in my room to work with her work in the world. Her role in the future will be an important one because before she ever set foot in a career guidance service, on the advice of her therapist at the time, she had made the decision to live rather than die. The deep work was going on; now the work of being engaged in a job that suited her had to be found.

'My grandfather was dying; he was a deeply spiritual man. He saw I was stressed out running my own business. The recession was coming. I put my heart and soul into my business and had it for eight years. I had great ideas, and I followed them through. 'I had opened my own business, had a baby, bought a house all in the one year.'

Eight years later the business was closed. A few years after this she lost her home. But this is nothing for someone like Eva – who has achieved serenity through endurance and decisions to be all she can be. She had her daughter to support, protect and see through. So she did what she has always done. She began again.

The very worst of her life had already occurred.

In her seventeenth year, all of her beauty was taken away by a key incident which needs no description here, but left her feeling worthless, lost and as she describes it as: 'Tumbleweed drifting through life.'

Previous to this her mother, who is mentally ill, had engaged in acts of cruelty, acts that the mother that Eva has become, would kill to prevent happening to her own daughter. Yet she accepts her mother's illness and has come to care for her, an indication of how far on the path of forgiveness some have to walk.

As she talks about the moments that made her entirety, I am often aware I am in the presence of light working for itself, bringing a pained and tormented time to a resolve. It would be foolish to say after what Eva went through that the pain will end completely, but it has been turned into something beautiful, a quest to find the meaning of life through her work.

'When I shut my business doors for the last time it was because I couldn't stand working with people's appearances anymore. I was helping people to look great, but as time went on, I saw they were spending huge amounts of money on things that weren't going to fix them. The work needed to be done on the inside.'

Eva wears the emblem on her inside forearm of her own freedom. It is a true representation of her. This is the emblematic statement from her in my perception of her.

She wants freedom, and she wants to be the best person she can be. Her physical appearance was always going to attract a legion of potential husbands or partners. She helped people with theirs, but ultimately the seeker in Eva, who saw her through the moments of torture she endured, was awake to the fact appearances change and age, but spirit develops and brings.

She felt like tumbleweed, but she was growing strong roots and being the force of nature that she is, has returned to education and opened the doors as part of that process.

If she knew what she was to become at 42 years old, would she as a young person have considered it possible? What was Eva like at 22?

'In a haze, I cast myself as tumbleweed going through life. The only other way I can describe it was that I met so many people but I never actually saw them or knew them. Now if I see people from that time I get embarrassed, wondering what they thought of me back then because I was going through a really hard time.'

This is evidence of the self-recrimination Eva is still working so hard to eradicate. 'I wished that I had done it differently. But I am doing it differently now.'

Her errors came from a response to her environment. Her responses to help herself overcome the errors and events, have created the woman who comes to me for careers counselling today.

'I agree. I wouldn't be the strong, driven survivor I am today. At the same time, I find it difficult to recognise that and use it as a tool for greatness. I can only go through one day at a time. It's the only way for me still.'

Forced to endure a violation, she had to make sure it came to an end. Then she had to become the adult supporting herself in the aftermath. It all became too much. By the time she was 18, she had made her first attempt at suicide.

'I took the tablets and was lucky I was found.' As she speaks, you can see it is bringing up a lot for her. Even coming to talk about her time with me, having been through the guidance process and made her changes, was difficult. 'I turned around, but then it became too much again. I was completely alone at this time. There was no one to help me.'

Still, despite seeing the bigger picture, she can sometimes feel shame for her way of being at the time.

'I don't like going back. It's very painful. I make excuses for my behaviour as a person. I hate being like that. I would like to be confident, come across as put together. I go through life as a broken person.'

The very thing that Eva describes herself as wanting to come across as is, who she is. Her brokenness is her making. She is not only a survivor but a thriver who can't yet give herself permission to see how much of an impact she makes in her gentle and beautiful person. She is a persuasion.

There is no doubt she has been through events which damaged and yet she herself can't damage, won't even. All she wants is to work with people who need the benefit of what she has survived. She is a born teacher and listener. Her main thrust in her training is towards education, but there is a strong counsellor in the making, rising in her vision of herself today which she will make happen in her tomorrow.

Shortly after the worst incident of her life, she came home to sit the Leaving Certificate the following year, and there was no possibility of that going well. She was in post-traumatic stress not just that year but for years after. It did not alleviate, and with little support, she made the attempts to take her own life.

The irony is while this emotional despair was being carried out she was carrying through on a career front in a manner that many would find admirable and most would find difficult.

But it still has to be pointed out to her somewhat that while the path was full of broken glass, the woman in the making was picking her way through the shards and still finding horizons. It is an unqualified strength and exhibited in compassion and concern for others, for her mother in particular.

'Still to this day I deal with my mother. When she was well, she would tell me about my father and become a mother. But she was too sick to take care of me. My grandparents, who took over my care, could not look after me 24-7. Things happened that should never have. Then when I met my father things happened that broke my trust completely.' In life, in mind, and in herself.

If Eva is an example of anything it is that we are not the self-hatred we feel when we have been taught unworthiness, or that we are unlovable. She couldn't have accomplished what she has, without having a greater self to be the custodian of the damaged and frightened child and teenager.

In her descriptions of herself, she talks about wearing the 'cloak' of capability, but it is evident to those of us who have the privilege of working with and helping her, that it is genuine ability.

A lot of my work with Eva has been to get her to go towards the goal anyway, despite her frequent sense of undeserving. I then ask her to put her feelings of self-loathing in context, to say they are based on past response to past experience and with her in moments but no longer all the time.

This combination of future focus and present self-regard is what she is a beautiful combination of. Eva worked in the beauty industry, and now she is learning to accept she is beauty itself. She is working for inner change to create a beautiful entirety.

There are moments when she needs help. She has had an experience early in the life, of the absolute worst one human can do to another, but by nature, she is able to negotiate.

'Sometimes in life, I can't vocalise how I feel. I am a submissive character. I let the loud person be the right one. In the last two years of college, there are always louder people in the classroom. I have an opinion but don't feel qualified to say.'

She is brave enough now to bring the past up. She is honouring her pain but it is not all of her now. There is a sun around her. So much potential being reached, no longer ahead of her, but here and being lived.

'I know that I have got something to give. That's why I went back to college; I want to do something I love. As a beautician for many years and coming towards the end, when I was deciding I didn't want it anymore; I was sick and depressed; it had a turning effect, I wanted to say to people, they had to go inwards.'

She saw she was beautifying the façade of painful souls but not solving anything. The clients were mostly women with plenty of money but lots of issues.

'I had to walk away.' This is a phrase I often hear in my room.

Life took away her house, which she had nested in for ten years. For a period all she had was her daughter and her decision to make sure she had all the chances Eva herself had been deprived of. Ironically this terrible period was a time when she was meeting the love of her life but didn't know it. He was picking her daughter up every day to take her to school.

'He kept her safe for a year; I used to put her in the car and put her seatbelt on, and on the last day I said to him thank you for looking after my daughter for the year.

'Later on, he got in contact with me and asked me to dinner. When we sat down to dinner he put a present on the table; I got worried as I didn't want someone who made too much effort. I opened up the gift, and it was a pink alarm clock, as I was always late and chasing after the bus down the road.'

It was the beginning of a full conversation. They just knew it would work and for the past four years, they have been together through thick and thin. He has encouraged her:

'He raised me up rather than put me down. He made me feel lighter in every decision and supported me no matter what.'

Together he and Eva have helped her to get back into education. She has negotiated her arrears for business and mortgage loans, cleared the practical issues

'My house, it was very hard to lose it. I had planted the trees in the garden when my child was born. It is huge now. I still can't bear to drive by it. It protected us for ten years.'

Beginning again with nothing is a familiar journey for Eva. She is dynamic. She is building up strength and progresses quickly at anything she sets her mind to fully, though she cannot acknowledge this fully in herself just yet.

'You'd look at me and wonder how I can drive a 53 seater coach.' But having heard her life story, you would not doubt it. She is referring to her own appearance, which is slight and feminine. 'I am so opposite to all of that. I love getting my hands dirty.'

She is not about doing her nails. Her desk is full of documents at home. She has successfully completed two years of a modular degree. In two more she will be a graduate and then she has full intentions of being a counsellor.

If she ever loses her house again, this woman can and would learn to build one with her own hands. The only reason she still needs career guidance is she doesn't yet fully trust her capability to have and succeed at the job she truly wants.

The compulsion is to believe she is not worthy yet. But that is being eroded in every conversation. She is naturally a winner, and no obstacle in her future will be as vast, awful and overwhelming as those she faced in childhood and early adulthood.

As we summarise her working life, going back over her changes and decisions, Eva has moved from filling up tissues to full eyes dancing with the joy of listing her achievements. Her daily decisions as a worker, business owner, mother and partner, to overcome losing her business, home, and to fight for her very life, have turned her into an embodied evidence that change can occur out of any circumstance.

She still harks to what people think, but the vibrant seeker within her has already moved away from outer perceptions towards inner questions.

This is one of the most important elements I want readers to get from witnessing her passage through life. You are always more than you ever even imagine yourself to be. You are capable of achieving your full dream and full potential as long as you are willing to work like Eva works. Every day she faces the kind of fears that used to cripple her, now she thrives on the challenges her huge range of life experience has given her fuel to face:

'People try to put me into that category. I told my boss I want to be challenged. I want to drive a big bus because I am not a wimp. If there is a job to be done, I want to do it. I love it, but I still suffer from anxiety.'

This is something I dispute with her. She won't relax into her success. Her anxiousness is a fear that the love she has found, the education she is paying for, the business she ran, the daughter she raises are all indications of her huge potential. She is afraid the horror and betrayals, the debts, the trauma she faced, will come again.

We can never go back to the start of our story, to the event itself, only to the last telling of the event. I advise Eva, as her counsellor did so successfully, that she is now telling her story with full support and to people who will do all they can to keep her safe which is what she does every day now, for her family unit, her community and her passengers. I smile as she tells me:

'This morning I was picking up junior infants, they are tiny. I put on all their seatbelts. I keep them safe.' This is the image of her I have. Keeping her own junior infant safe, the child she was, so unsafe, now ensuring the safety of all the other little children.

It is often the people from the worst backgrounds who become the biggest successes. A vulnerable and fragile young woman became a strong woman who lives close to her tears. The darkest of pasts is being turned into the brightest of futures.

If she decides on an illustration for her other forearm, it might be a full heart. She wears hers on her sleeve and in a strong way. There is no longer a sense of breakdown in Eva, but a breakthrough. She has put the splinters, the fragments of herself, into a full future.

This is the part she shares with my next client – Anna. The future cannot be seen entirely. But if you keep walking it arrives.

Eva will finish out the education she fought hard to achieve and works hard to maintain. She will continue to drive that huge bus and love the great man who came into her life, with a full understanding of herself. She will love her daughter enough to be a great example and will find her next road in the caring professions of listening to others who are beating their way out of the tangled, thick forest she once battled. She is in a clearing. There is more forest to come, but there are roads through this one, and she will follow them with her fully developed instinct and focus. I am privileged to work on that with her.

Teachers are from Jupiter; Pupils are from Mercury.

Sometimes you don't know how a capable person becomes overwhelmed, but for the young, a lot of work goes into understanding how the world works. Sometimes they get the message 'they are not what they think they are'. Unfortunately, adult realisation and the child's equivalent don't correlate. The magnitude of a teacher's impression on a child's mind can be enormous. Like the largest planet in the solar system expecting the smallest to engage in a task it finds easy, but the little planet sees as gargantuan.

All most primary school children want to do is well. Sometimes they look like they can manage things that are tearing them apart inside.

One of the people I have enjoyed working with is Anna – she is intelligent on all levels, and her uncertainties don't seem to be visible to the outsider. She is all she appears to be. The substance is there to back up *the someone*, in other words.

But a key event in her past led her to a level of performance anxiety no young person should go through. A high achiever she picked up the right pieces of paper, but now she fits the profile of the thirty-something who knows the right career is about finding the work that suits the person. Her school history, following a cataclysmic event in primary school, became about doing well without necessarily feeling well.

Her journey has been about putting her own personal preference to the top of a long list of previous achievements. It has not been easy to reclaim the identity she felt was taken from her, but she is brave, forthright and shows a natural ability no experience can take away. Here is the story of her reclamation in her own words:

'I never got a bad school report. Teachers seemed to think that I was hardworking and conscientious. I remember it because I had to ask Mam what 'conscientious' meant. She said she never had a problem in getting me to do my homework; I just did it. I had a grand time in school up to Fourth Class; wouldn't say I loved it, but it was grand.

I found out that I was going to Miss F's Fifth class. Miss F was different to the other teachers. She always had the banter with other students.

'This is right up my alley.' I remember saying to myself.

Things did not turn out the way I thought. Early into that school year, we were told that each of us would be writing a book for a competition in Waterford at the end of the year. We could base the book on anything we wanted. It could be a single storyline or multiple short stories. I remember feeling overwhelmed as she explained it to us.

Write a book? I could barely string a sentence together. I was not good at this sort of stuff. She gave us very little guidance. I got really stressed out by the whole process. I got worked up most evenings and cried and cried so much my skin would have blotchy red patches, and I would be worn out.

I spent so long writing these stories in the evenings that by the time I got to the rest of my homework, it would be very late at night, often ten or eleven at night. I remember going to bed after midnight one night at the weekend after much encouragement from Dad. But I started getting really pedantic about my other subjects.

The whole year was so stressful, not just for me but for my family too, as everything had to be done to the best of my ability. No shortcuts were allowed. I got so anxious and distressed when I couldn't figure something out or understand something. I was underweight, not eating and distressed most evenings.

The school had taken over my life. I stopped singing, dancing, playing camogie and being fun. I became a really serious child and very sensitive. I felt so bad that I was upsetting my family. It consumed everyone, something I still very guilty about to this day. Sometimes I feel my siblings hated me for the person that I was.

Things got so bad during that year, that Mam and Dad approached the school principal with my siblings. I did not find out about this until years later as I was not there. My teacher would not attend the meeting. They also brought me to a psychologist in Waterford for an assessment. I remember being in a room with paper and colouring pencils and him asking me to colour onto the paper the colour I would see when distressed.

I was thinking, even at that age, what has this got to do with anything?

I just used a red colouring pencil, as I thought red was the colour of anger and that should fit the bill. I got nothing out of that one off session. I then went to a counsellor in Dublin for a while. She was nice, but again I didn't get why I was there. She gave me exercises to do which I only ever did in the van on the way to Dublin with Dad.

I always felt my stress was circumstantial and I never really got a diagnosis or explanation for my symptoms. I was so glad to finish that year and hoped that Sixth Class would be better. Luckily it was. I had a lovely caring teacher, and I thrived again. I met a close friend that I am still good friends with to this day and the consistent crying over homework lessened a lot. I would still panic over homework that I could not figure out and would spend ages trying to work it out. I would often get overwhelmed at exam time and wanted to get the highest mark I could. However, I got back to playing sports and was in much better form. That time in Fifth class has had a lasting effect on me to this very day.

The effects of that year followed me and surfaced through ongoing exam stress, while essay writing overwhelmed me. I convinced myself I wasn't good at it. I wanted to do very well in the Secondary School Entrance exam as I really wanted to get into the top class. I felt anything else was beneath me and meant that I was slow or stupid. Imagine! Crazy, but that is how I thought.

The beginning of the first year was difficult. I remember feeling that the speed of the class was too quick for me and I would often not be able to keep up, especially in maths class. This overwhelmed me. I would often try and get ahead in the textbook so that I felt more relaxed in classes. As you can imagine, I hated English, so I ended up getting grinds in English for both the Junior and Leaving Certs. There were occasional nights still where I would cry over my homework. I would spend most of my free time after school doing homework and then all weekend doing homework. School took up a huge chunk of my life.

In examination years I stressed myself out studying. My aim wasn't to learn but to get the highest marks I possibly could. I never competed against my classmates; always against myself. I did well but for a price – my health. I felt sick opening my results. As soon as I found out I did well the focus was already on the Leaving Cert, getting four hundred points. I thought anything less would make me look stupid.

All I was focused on was getting good marks. When it came to filling out the CAO forms, Mam was really helpful, but I had no clue what I was interested in. I was good in a few subject areas, so I put down business and nursing to get it out of the way and forgot about it. The sixth year was a stressful year for me. It came to the week of the Leaving Cert, and I was wound up. Stressed and worried to my eyeballs, despite having worked hard for two years solid. I had no appetite and studied for long hours without taking a break.

The exams went reasonably well until the last day. I had business studies and biology on the same day. Business studies were my strongest subject, and I was relying on it to get me high points. However, in the exam I blanked. I remember the girl beside me (who wouldn't have been strong in the subject) scribbling away. The more I got my knickers in a twist, the more I could not concentrate. I didn't even finish the paper. I just wrote bullet points to scribble something down. I was a total mess when I got home for lunch. I bawled my eyes out. I cried and cried. I felt sick.

Mam tried to calm me down considering I had another big exam in the afternoon. I ate nothing that lunchtime despite much encouragement from Mam. Luckily my biology exam went really well for me which made me feel heaps better. The Leaving Cert was over. I said to myself, never again. What a brutal, brutal exam. It took everything out of me and all for what – points!

It's like my life was put on hold for two years. I worried a lot that summer about the results and how many points I would get. I remember saying:

'As long as you get over 400 points you'll be happy.'

I was away on holiday when my results came. My older sister came to meet me at Arrivals with the results in her hand. I felt sick. But she was smiling:

'You've done amazingly well.' She had counted up my points. I got 525. I was thrilled. I remember her saying:

'The world's your oyster now.'

I said straight away to myself that I did not want to pursue either of the courses I had on my CAO form, so I decided to take a year out. I came to this decision very quickly. As I write this, I am thinking how strong I was in my convictions and didn't care what others would think of this. I just thought: there is no way I have any interest in those courses, so my only option was to take a year out. Mam and Dad were okay with this. Mam said it was okay as long as I would be going to college the following year. It was encouraged to go college in our family. My older siblings had gone on. I don't think any of them overly liked what they did, but then again does anyone really know at that age? So, I went to work on our local newsagents. A girl I worked with was also taking a year out. We formed a very strong friendship and are still close. As it turned out, we ended up going to the same university the following year and lived together.

Before that, I took three months to do voluntary work in Ecuador, South America. I spent most of my time there on conservation sites in the rainforest. What an experience. It was tough at times, and I felt really exposed to the big bad world. I noticed that I had very little confidence in myself and felt I had nothing to talk about to the other volunteers. All the British volunteers that I met seemed to speak so well. They were knowledgeable and confident. It intimidated me, to be honest. I often cried and missed home, but perhaps some of that is normal at the age? Before I left for Ecuador, I completed the painful CAO again and again had no clue what I wanted to do.

I was very sporty at the time, so I chose Sports Science and Health in DCU as the modules were the only ones that really appealed to me. I like playing sports and would have liked human biology and health. It was my only choice I think on the CAO as it gave me a base from which to choose a more definitive career path.

At the time I think I was happy. I was looking forward to going to college to see and experience what it had to offer. I spent four years there. I found it hard to settle. I would spend much time thinking about what people in my year thought of me. I definitely was not in with the in-crowd, but then again I didn't want to be at the same time.

To the outside, this would not have been obvious, but I felt it on the inside. It's like college life didn't suit me. I would go to lectures but other times I would not. I found it hard to concentrate in lectures so would often print off loads of lectures notes prior to exams and cram. I was good at it, but cramming came with a lot of stress and tears at times. I remember crying over the assignment for an entire weekend not knowing where to start. Writing assignments stressed me out. However, as years went on I got into the style of writing, and so they became easier. Everything took me a long time as I would perfect it as much as I could.

Again, college work took up a lot of my headspace. Now don't get me wrong I still played camogie and socialised, but I would be extremely disciplined, and I would again lose weight due to lack of appetite and worry. I would often have a part-time job that I would quit right before exams as they were more important to me and I needed all the free time I could get. All my free time was used by studying or assignments. I was not good with time management. The pattern of the primary school fifth class had followed me into the fourth year of university.

As the end of the year approached a fellow student started talking about further study. Similar to the CAO, I had not given this much thought. I had not considered what I would like to do after I finished. Again I was so focused on getting good results, but for what, I didn't know.

I did well and took up an internship which was awful. I then found myself applying for a course in Dietetics at the undergraduate level in the UK. Why did I choose it? I panicked, and because I felt dietetics had a nice status, well, it fitted the bill.

I didn't like the idea of jumping straight into a more advanced course in nutrition without knowing the basics. I got a First in my first degree and remembered passing it off as if nothing happened. It didn't matter to me. My sister asked if I was happy and I was like: 'I guess.'

I had moved already in my head, to the next thing, which was a course in the UK. The future focus was all I ever worried about.

Mam and Dad came over with me to help settle me in. That was in 2006. What the hell was I doing? I didn't know what I was getting myself in for. I had no clue about the course and job, but I felt I couldn't admit this to myself or my family. I thought I had no other option at the time and another year out was not an option for me; well that's what I was telling myself anyway.

I needed to progress, so I told myself this was it! I still remember sitting in my dorm room with my suitcases thinking: I'm alone. I had lovely housemates and met some lovely people on my course, so I just got on with things. I didn't hate my course. I had some interest in it alright. Some modules were difficult, but I think the fact that I had done a science-based degree already I didn't find it overly taxing. Mind you I gave myself plenty of time to write my assignments, but I was definitely more balanced. I worked part-time at the time and had plenty of craic. I went out a lot and felt I was now living the student life I didn't allow myself to have in Dublin.

Academia did not overly stress me, but I did stress over work placements and worrying whether I had made people ill, though my parents were quick to reassure me that I hadn't. I seemed to get through them very well. I found out I got a 2. 1 in my second degree and I didn't care.

I had a big fat loan sitting over me, and the bank was pressing to start making the repayments, so I knew I had to get a job in dietetics. It was at that point that I realised that I did not fancy working as a dietician but I couldn't admit that to anyone.

My friends that I had studied with had all gotten jobs by this stage, and I remember panicking thinking: Sort yourself out. I got a job in Liverpool, and I was delighted, partly because I knew I had a steady job now to pay off my loan, not because I was excited to start working as a dietician.

I was afraid to start working properly. I would have had very little confidence in myself. I worried a lot. I would often be looking up things on the weekends worrying that I had made a wrong decision for a patient. It was a busy role. Similar to university, I met nice people and went out a lot. Work filtered into the background. I dreaded Sunday nights though. Perhaps most people do. I hated having to chat when all I wanted to do was stay quiet. I hated asking people about their weekends. It was so forced. I had little to no interest in small talk.

I just wanted to get on and do the job at hand. I would often say that people annoyed me (especially when I had work to do) and wished I worked alone. After two years as a junior general dietician, I applied for a more specialised position and was successful. We were well staffed so never overly stressed, but man did I get bored of that job. It was the same thing day in day out.

I returned to Ireland when I managed to secure a position as Senior Dietitian in a Dublin hospital. I thought it would be different. All I can say, in a nutshell, is that it was two years of hell. I went into a role where I was in over my head, with very little support and a huge workload. Both the staff and patients were demanding. I worried a lot about decisions I'd made in my downtime. My life outside of work became largely dominated by work. I would discuss the job relentlessly.

The last three months prior to making the decision to take a career break got particularly bad. I cried most nights discussing things every day with my fiancé. I was worried about leaving work as we recently bought a house and mortgage repayments were hanging over me.

I was desperately searching for a way out and was job hunting to the point of illness, but nothing was coming my way. My fiancé often encouraged me to take breaks from job searching as it was driving me nuts. Then, one evening on the train journey back from work, I thought of an old friend of mine who would be able to point me in the direction of a good careers guidance counsellor.

She mentioned Seamus Whitney. I had previously attended Seamus for careers guidance on my year out after the Leaving Cert. I had a vague recollection of that first meeting with him. So I contacted his office in Enniscorthy and took the next available appointment. I was made up – someone to help and guide me a little when I felt really low. So I turned up at Seamus's office on that Friday morning expecting him to do some assessments on my interests and that we would be talking about other potential career paths by the end of our session.

Put simply; the entire session was so far removed from my expectations. Seamus firstly asked me about my childhood / upbringing as he said that adults that come to him for careers advice are often in search of something else or that there is something else at the root of their unhappiness in their jobs. Well, I started talking and didn't stop. Then came the tears! It all just poured out. Then he asked me in his quiet, calm voice:

'When was the last time you took a deep breath?'

He was so right to say this. I was a ball of anxiety. I couldn't see that at that time.

I got so much more from that session than I had ever imagined. Seamus was and is an amazing man. He listened to me for much of the session and allowed me the non-judgemental space to speak and express myself. I felt like we got to know each other very well that day, almost instantaneously. I discussed with him the idea of taking a year out of work which he agreed with. He said I needed to take time to rest. I was again saying things like:

'I don't need to rest. I need a new career.'

He did ask me if it was my work environment or the profession that I disliked, and at the time, I didn't know. Seamus offered to guide and support me as a life/careers coach on my year out, and I jumped at the chance. I felt he was holding his hand out to help me to jump off the hamster wheel I felt I had been on for far too many years.

I felt so good leaving his office that day. I really felt great and uplifted as if a huge weight had been lifted off my shoulders. I knew I had huge support from Seamus. I often wondered why he offered to take me on, but I didn't care at the time. I felt things were going to start changing for me. I can't explain it but had so much belief in him and knew he would help me.

In the following few months, I met with Seamus every two weeks or so. I would travel to Wexford from Dublin each Wednesday evening and always looked forward to every session with him. I knew what to expect. He had me interested. Those sessions did not focus on career but rather on Anna, the individual. Seamus started saying to me:

'Who is the real Anna?'

As time unfolded Seamus introduced me to the spiritual path and I can say I will never look back. I went with it wholeheartedly. If you had said to me six months ago that I would be praying and handing over my worries to a Higher Self, I would have laughed. It has changed my view of the world.

I had a panic attack the night before my last day at work, at Christmas. I was in a state worrying about the quality of my work with one particular patient. I was a mess, although I didn't really see it. I am a perfectionist and expected nothing less than my best. I didn't allow myself to make mistakes.

The transition to the year out, in the January, was difficult. Seamus was supportive. He had gone over and above his duty. We were becoming good friends. He was with me every step of the way. I knew he was always on the end of the phone. It was extremely comforting. In March of that year but I got a part-time job at an outdoor adventure centre as an activity instructor, and so I felt I was on target. I continued to meet Seamus but less often, perhaps once every two months or so but often more on the phone than in person.

Over this time he taught me more and more about spiritual practice. I got a lot from it and took to it like a duck to water. It's like it was meant to come my way at this time. As I reflect on the past few months, I think my search for a career I like, is still there, but the focus is now more on finding my real/inner self. I believe that finding this out will guide me towards my true outer life purpose rather than the mind's wants and desires. It will then be more in sync with the real me.

I am at the midway point of my career break, and I have been granted another year leave of absence from my old position. My friends and family closest to me and most importantly my husband to be, say that the old, fun Anna is back. I am definitely more relaxed, grateful for the positive and not so positive things in my life. I try to see them all as blessings, and that I have something to learn from all of them.

I know I have a big heart and try to show more compassion to myself and not just others. This is a really difficult one as I am very self-critical. I am trying to be more mindful and meditate and adopt a regular spiritual practice. As for my future career, I am trying to take each day at a time and allow the divine design of my life to unfold. I struggle big time with this as I have zero patience and always want to know now! I plan to meet with Seamus next month to have a more formal discussion regarding jobs/careers for next year.

As Marianne Williamson says:

'When the real you shows up for work; real work shows up for you.'

I do know one thing for sure. I would have been lost without Seamus Whitney. As corny as it sounds, I feel he has helped to rescue me. He was definitely sent to me at the right time in my life. He has been there one hundred percent in my darkest, lowest moments and gave me the right words and listening ears at the right times. He has been a loyal mentor and spiritual guide to me. Just knowing that he is at the end of the phone gives me great comfort as I continue to put one foot in front of the other on this human journey of mine.

Seamus, I thank you. I am and will be forever grateful for crossing paths with you'.

10
THE CARPE DIEM QUESTION

Chapter 10

The Carpe Diem Question

Who's Day to Seize?

To laugh often and much; to win the respect of intelligent people and the affection of children- to leave the world a better place- to know even one life has breathed easier because you have lived. This is to have succeeded.
Ralph Waldo Emerson

 The last chapter of this book is a question. In the previous chapters, you have read about archetypes, defined your parameters and read a little of yourself in other people's lives. You have quantified your issues and created your sense of what could be if you could overcome or come to terms with them. You are beginning to guide your career.

The work is only just starting. Career guidance is not career delivery. True guidance comes from the place of experience – a combination of cerebral awareness, keen listening and spirited belief in the powerful effect of even small changes– but also takes into account your right to have your own experience.

For every person on our planet, there is a different way. We can have equivalency but never uniformity. My lessons have been forged by my life and its experiences. My consultative process is fashioned in the knowledge that when you leave this book or my office, you are going into your own territory to take your own route.

Chapter 10 – The Carpe Diem Question

Carpe Diem is the cry across the centuries. But you can end up seizing the wrong day, if you align with instincts not your own and let the global economy take you too far from your own sure ground. You might achieve the success that was never meant for you and know the failure of your own desires.

If there is one prevailing message in this book it is that you have to know who you are, define your passions and team this awareness to plans that take you towards your possibilities. You have to be flexible with your forward thinking and planning. Allow for life's changes and accept them. But the changes need firm rooting in your choices. Why?

Your life is linked to your work. If one is taking your personal identity, the other will be affected. In a society where 65 percent of the jobs school leavers will do have not even been invented yet, it is powerfully obvious that working choices are opening up all the time.

However, the choices are often tsunamis, overwhelming individual instinct, calling for increasing non-description. The human encounter is being eradicated. Anyone who has used an automated query service instead of being dealt with by a person will know this. How many times have you had to enunciate *yes* or *no* in a mid-Atlantic accent to get the right computerised response?

We work in a world of KPI's, ROI's and MBA's. You might not know what these initials mean, and if you do, you might not know what other ones mean. What has occurred in a world where specialisation is the prerequisite is that we often miss the bigger picture. Niches act like trenches when wider perspectives are not taken. We are a global species – not a global economy,

Where the higher human needs are answered is rarely around a board table but often in the private moment where the individual reflects on their individuality and makes clear choices based on a commitment to their self-discoveries. You've had the frustration of the automated phone lines, but what of those who work at the end of all numbered options?

People are being lured into giant call centres where they are paid to bear the brunt of the huge level of frustration and anger that we carry now as a species. Doctor's waiting rooms are packed with sick patients, often caused by work-related stress. Many current

173

workers are just about able to survive on a diet of coffee, *Red Bull* and processed foods.

I learned recently that our ancestors would not recognise the majority of the ingredients that we call food today. We have lost our individuality, our uniqueness and our creative nature, and all to line the pockets of faceless investors who use the ordinary man as a pawn in their game of how many billions they can make.

Those who do not take personal inventory and make choices based on their own minds can find themselves at the tail end of Taylorism. More on this later.

When our short working life passes by in the blink of an eye, we can be left with nothing, only pangs of regret. Nothing is worse than this. You have a right to express yourself. It makes an economy stronger, not weaker when its workers are fulfilling their own instincts. It makes sense as well as money to have a working life you enjoy.

In a country which lost so much of its talent through the brain haemorrhage of emigration, it is important to make sure it doesn't happen without emigration! We all have to do things we don't like, but the worst sin is people switching themselves off just to get the job done for their entire working lives.

Many people have traded the gifts they were born with and, sadly, much more aren't even aware of the gifts, talents and potential that they possess. Some will only ever use these talents as hobby pursuits, maybe one or two evenings per week. The thought of applying these talents in a work scenario is completely alien to them.

All too often, people are content with their lot and resigned to giving away their precious life in exchange for the money they need to support their lifestyle. When people finally become aware of this reality, it is often too late.

When my father drove me to the forerunner of Carlow IT, to register for a course, I had no natural disposition that he was doing his best. The car was an old reliable, and it got us there. The route was on old roads, and although it wasn't far, we took a road atlas with us so we wouldn't get lost. It took time. There was more time then. There were fewer choices. Now the economy has grown, the newest cars are equipped with Sat Nav and Bluetooth as standard, the route is mostly motorway.

Chapter 10 – The Carpe Diem Question

But the speeds and convenience of our new society are removing a history that offers us little time to self-determine on the conveyor belt between state exams and industry.

Everybody realises we now live in a world of constant change. The pace has dramatically quickened in the last sixty years since I was born. You don't need me to remind you how technology has impacted our lives and how our lives have subsequently impacted on our environment.

This summer a weekly staple of my home life over the sixty years, the local paper, stopped arriving. *The Enniscorthy Echo*, known locally as *The Echo*, had been around for twice as long as me. A history first printed in 1902 went into liquidation.

Dissolves such as these are dramatic, but change is a feature of all history.

For millennia, there was no apparent or immediate change in the world. Homo sapiens slowly evolved, and his main preoccupation was surviving in what was a hostile environment.

The concept of work as we know it now did not exist. Then, someone discovered fire. Warmth and cooked food came with this, and it must have felt like a revolution. Our brains grew at an alarming rate searching for the thing we did not know yet which could expand our universe. A wheel. A flint axe.

We took steps towards civilisation and our concept of identity evolved with each. As human existence became a little more sophisticated, specialised roles began to evolve such as blacksmith, weaver, shamanic healer and, to defend all of this newness, soldier.

At this stage, most work and skills were passed on from one generation to the next. Tradespeople began to emerge, butchering, baking, stonemasonry. The concepts and training stayed pretty much the same. Young people were shown the finer points of the trade by the master until they themselves had mastered the craft and were ready to use it to good effect in the world. Trained craftspeople like these were often highly regarded in the community and were in high demand. The stonemasons who constructed the Great Pyramids in Egypt were very well rewarded.

Around the time that Jesus of Nazareth signed up for his own apprenticeship in carpentry, the Romans had introduced the concept of money and coins, and we had our first international marketplace. A career for money rather than a barter arrangement came with the first coinage.

Cities were built, so the needs of the population were addressed by merchandise. Merchants such as Marco Polo took great risks to gain precious commodities in faraway China. Salt was like gold. Silk was fabric gold. Marco Polo was perhaps the first career celebrity outside of royalty or religion. He was exploring not for leisure, but profit. His pursuits made him famous and made his money.

Life-threatening at times, he still loved his task. Work was an extension of self. He was an exception rather than a rule. But he was fully representative of a growing concept, from the introduction of money, that if we pick a niche and exploit it if it suits us, if we are happy with what we do, or what we make, we can derive great fulfilment and satisfaction from it.

This model would pretty much last us for the next two thousand years, until the Industrial Revolution. A new dimension came to the workforce, peopled by visionaries who saw profitable possibilities in mechanisation. By the turn of the last century these masters of invention, these engineers, made a huge and lasting impact on the way human beings lived on planet earth.

Engineers gave us compasses to safely navigate the seas, steam to power our engines and machines to spawn an explosion in mass production. Everything from weaponry to surgery, from farming to fashion, could be done quicker and cheaper, making more money for unscrupulous owners. Wars and exploration carved the planet into territories. In everyday life, mechanisation was utilised to turn out a never-ending supply of items such as bicycles and Ford Model T cars.

The huge factories that produced these goods needed a constant supply of raw materials, often pillaged from around the world. They also needed labour, lots of it. People deserted their rural homelands in droves for the promise of a wage, less affected by seasons and circumstances. The dreams of possession came with the migration. They might own their own home, bicycle, car, at some stage in the future.

The truth was that the work was dangerous, dirty and not self-directed or determining. Processes, once natural, began to be organised into long lines of production. Workers completed endless repetitive tasks for days, weeks and ultimately years on end. They did what they were told, and they were paid, fed and housed. This concept was Taylorism. Managers think, and workers do. A new way of being in the world had come to existence.

For me, this was a very significant shift from the traditional, craft and trade based approach, as experienced by generations of our ancestors, to a system that still prevails, of people exchanging their time for money.

Taylorism is the dominant route or approach to work. Dressed up as a job for life or a job with prospects – whether it is with a State body or the lower echelons of Apple Inc. – it does not take into account the unique capabilities of individuals. In exchange for this, it takes care of basic responsibilities. Ironically in doing so, it removes the higher individual needs of self-determination and self-actualization.

While our methods of work may be more sophisticated, we clamour for careers that are seen to provide a reliable salary, opportunities to rise through the ranks and ultimately to earn more money. This may make financial sense to some, or even most, however, I believe many people have traded part of themselves to the big corporations and multinationals.

The company pays the going rate for the job. The workers themselves get very little or nothing other than this financial payoff. In some cases, they must work hours that are completely out of sync with their natural body rhythms. They are of course "compensated" for their time by being paid higher premiums. This is honey, and while it is a glorious substance, it also sticks and congeals if it isn't consumed properly.

The Lifestyle Trap

Many of my adult clients present to me, anxiously looking for positive change in their work-life balance. Before I even start to look at future possibilities, it is very important that I carry out an appraisal of what their current situation is in financial and family terms. Commitments such as mortgage repayments are often significant limiting factors to a person's ability to re-enter education, retrain or consider self-employment.

In a high percentage of cases, I feel people are actually trapped. They have been busy establishing a lifestyle that includes the house, car and holidays, and most feel that these are areas that cannot be compromised. This is the dilemma, and having seen it so often, I ask myself, why?

There are two major reasons. The first is we have become a victim of the very system we have created. We are the consumers as well as the makers of the mass produced.

In 1976 when I worked my first £20 a week job, Jackson Brown's famous song *The Pretender* was on the radio and in record stores. Every time I hear the words now and when I heard them then, they penetrate deep into my psyche, often with a tinge of regret for the kind of life many people have settled for. It's worth reviewing the lyrics:

I'm gonna be a happy idiot
And struggle for the legal tender
Where the ads take aim and lay their claim
To the heart and the soul of the spender
And believe in whatever may lie
In those things that money can buy
Thought true love could have been a contender
Are you there,
Say a prayer, for the Pretender
Who started out so young and strong
Only to surrender

Jackson Browne was wise to the matrix type world we lived in even then. His words are a stark warning to us all. Were we listening? Not at all! We have allowed the situation to become even worse.

In our *struggle for the legal tender,* we are controlled by highly creative, marketing and advertising campaigns, in turn, fuelled by giant media corporations. People are noticing now, that if they do a single Google search, they are peppered with adverts relevant to that search the next time they open their Facebook or Instagram accounts.

How this is all achieved is for another book, but we can't ignore it.

Chapter 10 – The Carpe Diem Question

Sadly, the results are all the same. We are constantly seeking for the next thing, sometimes on easy credit and to fund this, we are chained to the job. This is the matrix of the material world.

I'm going to rent myself a house
In the shade of the freeway
Gonna pack my lunch in the morning
And go to work each day
And when the evening rolls around
I'll go on home and lay my body down
And when the morning light comes streaming in
I'll get up and do it again
Amen

This situation is getting worse for our next generation. Young people live in a world of instant gratification. The one thing they haven't developed is patience. They are used to making quick decisions, which manifests products at a lightning pace. They are in such a hurry to have all the trappings of life: the mortgage, the car, the house and indeed the non-material things such as a relationship and family, that by the age of thirty, they are caught in the trap.

They are overloaded with the burden of debt, the snare of the modern lifestyle and caught in a prison of comparison. Then, it's often too late to undo. They try, but now they must operate within the confines of this material matrix. It's so sad.

What can we do? Indeed, can we do anything to stop this rollercoaster? At a time where we seem to be controlled by a system, we can examine our own individual choices. We can do it for ourselves, and we can also look at how our decisions influence those around us, including our children.

The treadmill of life today seems to be one of school, college, job and lifetime commitments to partners and mortgages. It's almost as if we can't wait to get into the burden of debt and responsibility, and then we spend the rest of our lives trying to extricate ourselves from these manacles.

This book features case studies because we all can learn from the examples of others. Some are people who have managed to stand up to the system, question what it's all about and find their true selves in that process. Yes, there are often sacrifices along the way to be made, but I do know when asked was it worth it, the answer was always a resounding *yes*. Invariably, the only regret expressed by any of my clients who come to me on the wrong career course and looking to put it right is:

'Why didn't I do it sooner?'

The only thing that keeps super rich and super greedy barons in place, is our pursuit of happiness through the acquisition of more and more material things. The Butcher, the Baker, has been replaced by the Corporate Freedom Taker. Freedom is freethinking; once you reclaim your right to think, you can reclaim your right to self-direct and in turn self-actualise.

We can stop ourselves being enslaved to corporations if we want to. All we have to do is recognise who we are, where we want to be and what part of society we wish to belong to.

We need to guide our careers and lives with the kind of impartial wisdom that is independent of fear and full of self-knowledge and enquiry.

We need to question everything about why we do what we do and who we are doing it for. We must seize the day and make it ours.

Website: www.whitneycareerguidance.com/

ABOUT THE AUTHORS

About the Authors

Seamus Whitney

In 1998 Seamus Whitney founded Whitney Career Guidance, an organization committed to helping others reach their full potential as Human Beings.

Whitney Career Guidance, specializing in Career Guidance, Training and Personal Development has helped many people reach their career and personal goals.

During that time Seamus developed his own unique way of assessing his clients and their suitability for various careers. Using these techniques he has built up a strong client base both at home in Ireland and abroad.

Prior to this Seamus had over 20 years' experience working in industry, the vast majority at senior management level.

As a training consultant he has worked with a broad range of companies including multi-nationals, indigenous Irish companies, public sector clients and Skills-Nett Training initiatives.

Seamus is also a qualified Life Coach and acts as Career Guidance Consultant for South East Radio.

Suzanne Power

Suzanne Power is a prize-winning author who has worked for over 30 years with words. She now mentors writers in business and academic matters, through Whitney Career Guidance.

Her novels, short stories, memoir, columns and poetry have been published internationally.

As an independent editor and mentor of professionals, she has worked with several high-profile authors to achieve and continue being published, together with numerous self-published projects.

She devised Maynooth University's *Creative Writing for Publication* and *Two Roads* programmes, helping many writers to win publication and awards, producing three anthologies with cohorts.

She has been editor of three consumer magazines and features editor of two national newspapers, an award-winning journalist and a national columnist for fifteen years in a range of titles. She is also a broadcaster, producer and researcher working for BBC, RTE and UTV.

Suzanne is a poetry therapy practitioner and has worked in therapeutic, and community settings, producing anthologies and offering both group and one to one writing support. Apart from her PTP qualification, she has a BA in Journalism and a Masters in Creative Writing.

Summary

Seamus Whitney, one of Ireland's top career guides, has observed human nature from a work perspective for over 40 years. His insights encourage, invest and invite workers to take action and make or find work that works for them.

A former HR high-flier he found his niche, taking risks and action to establish a consultancy where clients listen not only to him, but to themselves.

Today's marketplace means the average worker will have three careers. So proactivity is a prerequisite. Ditch the business slogans, find your personal vision, and pave the way to the work objective that most suits. Today's step will lead to tomorrow's outcome.

Written with author Suzanne Power, Seamus sketches the big picture making this book a must read not just for anyone working, but anyone focused on what it means to take an active part in society.

Guide your Career will get you thinking, acting, responding and working differently.

Make work, work for you.

"Seamus writes from the confident position that comes from studying and working at the source of the greatest educational authority of all, that of the lived experience. This book is insightful, accessible, full of good advice written in a style that combines narrative and anecdote with practical guidance for academic and career guidance. The one overriding impression that the reader will get from this book is to be prepared to go beyond what is merely expected and take the risk to seek to find oneself. It's an admirable challenge for us all." (**Dr. Derek Barter, Continuing Education Co-ordinator, Dept. of Adult and Community Education, Maynooth University, Maynooth, Co. Kildare. T: 01 708 3948, November 2017**)

"This book which sets out to offer practical careers advice is upbeat and nicely articulates the 'career life' trajectory. The discussion focuses around anecdotes and career dilemma scenarios that are easy to relate to, thus making it accessible and of interest to a wide target audience. In this book the 'career path' (whether referencing school leaver, young adult or older adult) is not viewed in isolation but rather as an integrational concept that takes us beyond just finding a 'career' to the realm of finding a career that is right for us, our personalities our characters and our value systems. I really liked this book. For me, it echoed the criticality of a career well chosen – 'doing what you love' – a career path that ultimately leads to the unveiling of the true and contented self. " (**Mary Bolger, Employer Based Training Co-ordinator, National Learning Network, Associate Lecture, Institute of Technology Carlow, also a Teaching Fellow with the UK Higher Education Academy, Nov 2017**)

Website: www.whitneycareerguidance.com/

Made in the USA
Columbia, SC
08 January 2018